Purpose

Making Sure Your Purpose Finds You

Sue Fitzmaurice

Published by Coven Tree Books

For Madison and Ruby,

Watching your purpose journey unfold
is the greatest thrill of my life.

Also by Sue Fitzmaurice

Fiction

Angels in the Architecture

Non-fiction

Purpose – the Elements of Purpose
The Accidental Mary Pilgrimage
A Month in the Himalayas
Billow & Breeze

Note to the Reader

In the main I employ *English* English. Those unused to this great language may stumble over the 'u' of neighbour and the verb of 'practise'. There is no word 'gotten' in the Queen's English and we politely 'minimise' without a 'z' (which we pronounce 'zed', by the way). Quotations from others are in the version of English of their nationality or first publication. Any other errors are indeed mine and I pray your forgiveness.

Contents

Introduction

Figuring out your purpose and getting to a point where you feel like you're living it is hard. Before you arrive at a fuller understanding of purpose generally, and your own in particular, it feels like a mystery – something almost magical, that's going to require some specialised knowledge that you don't imagine you'll ever gain. In the end it's incredibly simple and straightforward stuff; it's certainly not magical, and you'll wish someone had explained it to you much earlier because it would have saved you a lot of time and worry.

In my first book on Purpose, I explained the fundamental elements of purpose. In this second volume, I want to explain how to put yourself into the right situation and circumstances to allow Purpose to find you more easily.

We talk about *finding* our purpose, but it's really more that *it* finds us. And it does so when we're in the right space – the right vibration, the right set of circumstances, the right stage in our development – to receive it.

And when I say 'it', I don't mean a particular, singular thing – a job or a role (although that may be a significant factor for some) – but rather a path that you now journey on, that feels more authentically you. Your purpose isn't one thing, but a way of living that gives you meaning, and that has a sense of spirit about it for you. It may have the feeling of *this is what I'm supposed to be doing* or *this is what I'm here for*; it may feel like love or freedom; it *will* feel meaningful and purposeful. If finding what you're here for is important to you, then this is your life's journey. You may think you're just looking for the right job, but I'm almost certain that what you really want is much deeper and more meaningful than that.

Our purpose is not something that can be viewed in isolation from any other part of our life. It's not a nine-to-five activity that disappears in between office hours. Every part of our life impacts on it, and it impacts on every part of our life; indeed, it *is* our life.

And so because it *is* our life, and not a part of it, our task in making our purpose a reality is to create the right conditions in every aspect of our life, so that our life aligns with our purpose and becomes the best setting for our purpose to flourish.

This does not mean though that our purpose is something that happens in the future, out there somewhere, one day when the time is right. You start to become aligned with your purpose the moment you decide to do so, and whilst it may not feel like your purpose is happening straight away, or after a week or even a year, as long as you are working on creating the conditions for it to unfold, then it will.

It doesn't feel like an easy journey to start with, although you may well look back on the beginnings of it and realise it was a lot simpler than you thought. It will frequently challenge you to face up to things about yourself that you'd rather not. You may feel like you're being asked to take enormous leaps of faith that utterly terrify you. You will have to step outside your comfort zone. You may feel like you're risking everything. In my experience, the other side of every challenge or risk or leap of faith has always been a lot easier to get to once I'm there than I thought it would before I took the leap.

I've come to believe that our main task is not in *looking* for our purpose as such but clearing the obstacles that stop it from finding us. Living our purpose is the manifestation of our spiritual self, and necessarily our lack of attention to that part of our self means accepting it is challenging, as most of us have created all kinds of blockages to its free flow. Depression and anger, which often go together, are two of the biggest obstacles of all. Anything that is not of the spirit – judging others, not practising forgiveness and gratitude – inevitably has to be given attention and correction.

Many people are experiencing a sense of urgency about finding their purpose. It's very much a factor of a certain age – middle age especially – but it's also a factor of our development as a species. Our standard of living is high, we have exceptional levels of freedom, we have access to knowledge and information unheard of only 20 years ago, and we've reached dizzying heights in our careers and expectations. While that's all a marvellous adventure, many of us who've benefitted from all of these things have also come to understand that there wasn't the meaning and fulfilment inherent in many of them that we'd anticipated. And so we're looking for more. And *more* is no longer to do with acquisition, achievement or authority. Far from being about power and money, it's not even that much about knowledge (although that is a factor); it's about meaning. It's about being happy *all the time* and it's about knowing your place in the cosmos.

One of the expectations people have in wanting to find their purpose, is wanting to find the job that's right for them. If that's all you're looking for, then a careers counsellor will help. However, I can almost guarantee that whilst many people think this is what they want, in truth it's probably not.

What I find is that most people are looking for meaning, and to be able to do meaningful work, and for the opportunity to make a meaningful contribution. *Making a difference* and *giving back* are two things I hear a lot from my clients. Along with the idea that they believe they are here for a reason.

**He who has a 'why' to live for
can bear almost any how.**

Friedrich Nietzsche

What I also find is that when people are using these kinds of words, they've generally gone beyond the idea of 'job' and they know they're looking for something bigger than that. In various ways I can see that this is an aspect of people's spiritual views and their view of the world. There's an increasing awareness that the world has a lot of challenges and people want to make some commitment to healing it.

I also see that most people are not so clear where to start. Because they know if it was just about a job it would be a whole lot simpler; and that somehow, it's more complicated than that, but just how to think about it and where to start is beyond them. This is generally because we've never thought about it much before, if at all.

Nobody taught us about purpose.

School and university have tended to always be about *job* and *career*, and words like *purpose* weren't used. When we were little we were always asked *What do you want to be when you grow up*, and we were expected to answer teacher or fireman or lawyer or doctor or nurse or something else that was about a job or a career. No one ever asked **what would you like to be *like* when you grow up?** Or **what do you think you're *here* for?** Or **what gives life *meaning* for you?**

Some of us found *some* opportunity to explore this within religion, but religion is not always a guarantee of meaning, or possibly one's quest for meaning goes beyond one's religion. Maybe you find you have questions that your religion can't answer. And so, a broader *spiritual* exploration helps. (Of course, for many people these two – religion and spirituality – overlap a great deal, but equally for a great many they are quite exclusive of each other.)

And herein lies the problem with why purpose wasn't taught. It's fundamentally about spirituality. And modern education, sadly, doesn't go there. When we took Christian instruction out of school we threw the proverbial baby out with it, and any opportunity to include the language of spirituality within education. Even the concept of **finding meaning in work** hasn't caught on much within education yet, although it has started to enter the lexicon of modern business. It was certainly important to me when I ran various organisations to find out from staff what was meaningful to them and where they wanted to go in their work life.

I believe, as a boss, and especially as a parent, that one of **our primary responsibilities is to assist others to connect to their own purpose in life.** Of course, if we've no idea about purpose generally, or our own specifically, then we're less able to help others with theirs, most especially our children.

And so the hope arises: *there has to be more than this.*

This language of purpose is now being heard more widely, although for the most part our understanding of it remains limited. More and more people want lives they believe in. They don't want their lives to be about acquisition and achievement; they've realised that those things have only ever made them happy for about five minutes, or maybe a day, and then they want the next thing. And so the hope arises: there has to be more than this.

And then often rather late in the day we're finding ourselves in our middle age or our third age wondering what our purpose is, wondering if we still have time for it, maybe wondering at what we might suddenly even see as the pointlessness of so much else we've done before now.

The thing is, you've actually been on your purpose journey all along – you just didn't know it. Now you're becoming conscious of it. And it's not about whether you still have time for it – it's there as long as you are. And **nothing you've done is pointless** – it's all absolutely as it should have been and now you're going to find out how useful it all was. Now it's all going to start making sense, and now, finally, you're going to be having this conversation out loud, along with thousands and thousands of others, and between us we're going to make sure that those that come after us 'get' this.

1. What Purpose Isn't

When I was at university studying political science, I took a paper called 'Military and Society'. I was a bit of a hippie protestor and didn't think much of the uses the military were put to, so I thought it would be interesting and almost certainly fuel my youthful sensibilities. The lecturer probably knew this was most of us and spent the first lecture telling us what his paper *wasn't* about. It wasn't about the military industrial complex, it wasn't about the nuclear arms race, and it wasn't about a whole lot of other things as well.[1]

What I've realised over the years of researching purpose, and talking about it and coaching on it, is that there are a lot of things people think purpose *is*, that it just *isn't*. So I'm going to clear a path through a whole load of misunderstandings and I hope that's a good place to start to create a truer picture of what finding your purpose – or letting it find you – is all about.

It's not about a job.

Sadly, in our haste to abbreviate, simplify, and create a meme for everything, several diagrams of purpose have made their way around ~~social media. You've probabl~~y seen them. There are some with three

[1] It was about military-led societies – African and South American countries in the main, where there'd been military coups and the military was in charge. It wasn't anything I'd anticipated but it was very interesting.

outer rings, some with four like the one below, some where the circles overlap, some that include words like mission and career and passion, and so on. They're all almost completely wrong. Which is a shame, because I like a good model, and I'm all for simplifying things. But these do more than simplify – I think they get the concept of purpose completely wrong.

The problem with this model and others like it
is that it treats purpose as though it's just about the work you do.

These models are rudimentary and very introductory. And like a lot of very introductory things, a lot of people will look at this and think they know about purpose, and sadly they'll know hardly anything at all.

The problem with this model and others like it is that it treats purpose as though it's just about the work you do – your job or career. Purpose is about how you live your life – your work of course is a part of that – but when you get a bigger and better picture of purpose, you'll realise this is just one aspect.

Of course, we come to purpose very often via the idea of work, job and career. We're either in a career and feeling it's the wrong one, or we've not worked outside the home (at all or for some time), and all of a sudden, it's time. Alongside the idea of job, we do come at purpose looking for meaning, fulfilment, satisfaction and similar such things, but if we only take that as far as our job then we're not getting the fullest picture. It's like the difference between reading the dust jacket and reading the whole book. It's wonderful that so many of us are approaching our work with a view to meaning and satisfaction; that's certainly a step in the right direction, and it's hugely important. But there's more. So much more.

It's not an equation.

Another thing that's wrong with this model is that it looks at purpose as an equation, whereby if you somehow create a list of what you're good at and what you love, and somehow connect that to something that pays, and so on, then you'll get to x, being your purpose. And that's absolutely not how you'll find your purpose.

> Purpose is not an equation:
> $$Skill + Passion + Income \neq Purpose$$

Your purpose, once you find it, will probably have these elements (ie. that you'll love it, you'll be good at it, it'll make a difference), but they are a fraction of the total picture of your purpose, and some of them may even be absent, at least initially. Your purpose will possibly even be something you don't love to start with and may include things you've overlooked in the past because you don't like them at all. Or you think you don't like them. We can't reduce life and its key elements to an equation.

Another challenge of this model is that each of the aspects depicted are equal. This is never going to be the case. It's not $1 + 1 + 1 + 1 = 4$. If it's remotely equation-like, it's more like $0.5 + 1.6 + 0.1 + 2.7 + x + y + z = $ *a journey to an unknown destination.* Or in other words, an equation doesn't cut it.

No two people would have the same model of purpose, nor would any one person's model stay the same in any of its aspects for their lifetime. Purpose is not a static thing, such that once you've found it there you are. Your life is your purpose, and your purpose is your life; it evolves and grows and changes and you will be journeying along it until your last breath. And it's probably this factor in particular that redefines purpose from the social media meme: there is no end point.

Much of how we are socially engineered to manage our lives means that we aim for this point, and then the next point, and then the next point, and we plan our life to each point. Amazingly we can insist on keeping on with that model even in the face of overwhelming evidence that life doesn't work that way. As John Lennon said, *Life is what happens when you're busy making other plans.* Which of us can deny that reality? It's the way all our lives have unfolded, and yet we'll continue to push the proverbial uphill – and it begins to feel increasingly uphill – planning out the steps and stages of our lives. Purpose doesn't operate according to a plan that you thought up and maybe even wrote down. Purpose doesn't come from your mind or your thinking. It often runs, in fact, very counter to that part of ourselves.

The irony is – and I'll talk in more depth about the wonders of irony and contradiction further on – that of course we still must plan! We plan all the time. I haven't suddenly stopped planning my life just because I'm now living my purpose. Oddly even, a huge chunk of my year is already planned out as I write this, including travel to a dozen different countries through the course of the year and that absolutely needs a lot of planning. I plan my day, I plan my grocery shopping, I plan my social media and marketing. I have plans for my 'retirement', especially financial ones. (By retirement, I really mean when I get to that age where I collect a national pension; I don't really envisage retiring in any traditional sense.) I still plan. But none of my planning is in aid of getting to a particular point in my life as such. I don't have a career plan, and I certainly don't have any focus on achievements, at least not for their own sake. I don't have an equation: that if I do this, this and this, I'll get that, and then I can tick that box. I'm not about ticking boxes. I don't have any point that I *have* to get to. My life isn't *about* getting to any point. It's all about now, this moment. This is the complete opposite of what most of us have been encouraged to do in our lives, in order to create security. I'm not about security either – at least not in any traditional sense; more about that to come.

It isn't limited.

By now you'll be getting the idea that your purpose isn't one particular thing that you find, that then never changes. At the very least it changes and evolves in small ways every day, and your larger sense of purpose will shift also.

I've had at least half a dozen careers in my adult life, and around twenty jobs that I can remember off the top of my head. I've been variously aware my whole life, including as quite a young child, that I had a particular purpose as a spiritual seeker. Religion and spirituality have always fascinated me, and that aspect of my purpose will continue this whole life, I have no doubt. Few, if any, of my jobs or careers had anything to do with this specifically, although as a spiritual seeker you learn spiritual truths in everything you do. The urge to motherhood in my early to mid-thirties, and the very profundity of it still, have shown me this is a massive part also of who I am and what I do. I idolise my two children, which is

22

perhaps not always the best thing, but I am in awe of them. I'm far from the best parent, but nothing and no one has taught me more about myself. I'm not sure that 'mother' is a part of every mother's actual purpose, which is not a judgement of anyone's mothering ability or the depth of their experience, but at any rate it is definitely a purpose of mine – I *feel* it as purpose, as profoundly meaningful in a spiritual way. If asked to describe myself in half a dozen words or less, *mother* is generally one of them.

One of the very *me* things I discovered I always do in my work, whatever work I'm doing, is to bring people together, to create networks, groups, gatherings of like minds. With the advent of social media, and in particular Facebook, I've found a new and fun way to continue to do this when I'm no longer in a formal job or career role. *Social networker* is another of my purposes. When I combine that with spiritual seeker, I've found that sharing my learning manifests into my current role as writer, coach, speaker. Discovering this role of bringing people together was, in hindsight, a really important step in becoming aware of my purpose. It came about twenty years ago when I'd been asked to apply for a particular position with a national organisation I'd belonged to at the time. It was a prestigious position and I'd felt honoured to have been asked. But I had to write an application and I'd been self-employed for quite a long time by then, and hadn't applied for a job for ten years or more. When you're applying for jobs every few years, or you're in a position of interviewing others for jobs, then you get a mindset about resumés and so on. I was completely out of that mindset. So when I was writing this application I asked my husband *What am I good at?* because I couldn't think what to put; and my husband said *You're really good at bringing groups of people together to solve problems and make things happen.* I've never forgotten those words and they've come back to me time and time again. This is most definitely an aspect of what I do, of who I am, of my purpose. I love forming groups; I get a huge buzz out of it. So much so that it's rare I take on any new project on my own. If I could successfully write a book with someone else I would. And perhaps one day I will. I love coming up with an idea and finding others to do it with me.

These days I also describe myself as a traveller, which overlaps with the other aspects of my purpose, and occasionally, joyfully, with being a mother as well. To travel with my children is one my greatest thrills.

Most of all I feel I am *living my purpose* and *living purposefully.* My life feels full, joyful, exciting, and also very peaceful. I know what my purpose is, and it continues to unfold for me every day in new and often unexpected ways. And I'm open to whatever comes my way.

It's not a mystery that requires magical thinking.

Nearly twenty years ago, I took on an MBA – a Masters in Business Administration. I'd been in business most of my working life and I'd been thinking about doing an MBA for several years. It's quite a commitment, both in time and money, and it's quite an intense experience. I wanted to be clear that I was doing it for the right reasons. In the end, the biggest reason was that whilst I knew I had a lot of business knowledge already, I didn't have a framework that allowed me to make better use of what I knew. Of course, I learnt lots of individual things I didn't know already, but the most valuable thing I gained was the framework to hang all that knowledge on.

I know it may not seem like it, but as far as I can tell, everything about finding and living your purpose is actually really simple and ordinary. There is nothing wildly radical or magical about anything I talk about. Most of you will have heard most of it before. All I have done is put all that knowledge into a framework. You will have picked up many of these pieces of advice in many different settings but you may not have realised their relevance to your purpose. Most particularly you won't have put them into the structure and categories I have, making them more useful to you. The words aren't new to you, but the way I've put them together and the emphasis I've put on them, is.

I think key in this framework is to put purpose in the context of the spiritual, and also to grasp the spiritual as an inherent aspect of life, regardless of your own actual spiritual, religious or non-religious feelings and beliefs. This is foundational. It's not a mystery and it's not magical; it's simply understanding that the desire for purpose and meaning is a call from the spirit – it's not a call from your mind, or even your heart, although of course what is heartfelt has a close relationship to the spirit. It's a trap to pursue purpose with your mind and thoughts alone, without finding a place for the spiritual. You will lose purpose if your pursuit of it is largely the pursuit of career. Frustrations of not living your purpose will continue to dog you; they may feel put to rest for short periods but they will re-emerge. I'll talk about this aspect of purpose and spirituality a lot more, and hopefully in ways that aren't off-putting for those for whom spirituality hasn't been a thing.

It's not unknown to you.

In all likelihood, your purpose is not unknown to you. I can look back on my entire life, especially my working life, and see that it was all quite obvious really. That's the benefit of age of course, and also of someone who's spent a lot of time thinking about this. (The irony is that I can equally say *Well who knew it would go like that?!*) Most people I know who are living their purpose quite strongly, would I think say this same thing. The more you get clear on your path, the more you can see that it was there all along. Which does often lead to one rolling one's eyes and wondering why we hadn't seen it much earlier, but we do also have to accept that most of those obstacles and bad turns – not to mention bad directions – were all a part of the path. I have some reluctance to accept the idea that *everything is meant to be*, but like many such ideas it has elements of truth to it – it's not the whole truth, but it has some meaning just the same.

Hindsight's a great thing, and it's easy to say one's purpose was there all along. It's obviously not so easy to see at the time, since otherwise there wouldn't be so many people searching for it. But it reveals itself to us in moments of spiritual clarity, when we connect to our purpose, if only briefly. And as you get more firmly on your purpose path you will have a sense of familiarity about much of what you come across. That feeling of *This feels right!* will come up often. When you get that feeling, tune into it and become familiar with it. Try to summon it up at other times. The further along your purpose path you go the more you will experience this sense of familiarity with it. It's a unique and wonderful feeling, and very reassuring, and it acts to affirm your path. It brings with it a unique kind of happiness as well; it's very peaceful and feels like 'coming home'.

It's not tied to achievement.

This is a slightly tricky one because of course much that we may decide to do in our lives will require qualifications and training. I add this for three reasons: 1) as a caution, that your desire to gain certain experiences or qualifications isn't society-led, parentally-led, ego-led, etc; 2) there is a trap in seeking constant achievement – especially educational – as a tool for scanning the field for your hidden purpose, thinking the more things you try the more likely you are to find it; and 3) because in various ways the notion of achievement runs counter to purpose. The best way to explain this is to return to the foundation of purpose: that it is the manifestation of your Spiritual Self. I think it's probably easy to get that your Soul doesn't require qualifications. It doesn't require you to have been somewhere or done something. It's sufficient to itself.

You will not have a sense of living your purpose if your goal is just to get to the end of everything.

I read recently that New Zealand's beautiful walking tracks – in particular the very famous Milford Track, arguably the best in the world – are being overwhelmed by a massive increase in walkers, in some cases by over a hundred per cent more. A New Zealand Department of Conservation worker was quoted as saying:

A lot of people aren't interested in what is around them anymore… They are ticking off their bucket list and getting through it as quickly as possible. They have their headphones in, head down, get up on the pass, take their photos and the tick is over. People do have a lot

of different reasons for doing it ... but increasingly, people do it
because it has become a bit of a status thing.²

Doesn't that just say so much?! There's a world of understanding in there about the way in which many people are choosing to live their lives. Ticking off the mountains they've climbed, because it's the list that counts, not the actual climbing.

Last year I was doing a lot of castle-hopping around Scotland. I have a particular love for Scotland and its history and I immerse myself in it regularly. One very rainy, stormy day I was driving down the east coast from Aberdeen and stopped in to see Dunnottar Castle, which like many of Britain's castles is built on a very high, rocky and dramatic cliff jutting out into the sea. Sadly, the weather was so severe that the castle was closed. I wasn't especially deterred though and ventured out to the nearby cliffs, enjoying the remoteness of it and imagining, as I do, what it must have been like to live there all those hundreds of years ago in such harsh circumstances. As I teetered on one cliff to the south, I saw forty or so people wander down the path from the car park in a group, stop at the end of the path, take photos, and then head straight back up the path again. There were any number of mini adventures to be had even though the castle was closed, but not a single step was climbed down or up. *I* took a photo of *them*. After they'd gone I ventured down the north

² *'World's finest walk': New Zealand's Milford Track being spoiled by tourist hordes*, Eleanor Ainge Roy, www.theguardian.com, 21 January, 2018.

side to the beach, sliding down a muddy bank to enjoy crashing waves. Heading back up I slipped over – twice – and smothered in mud and greatly amused I headed back to the car park. I met a few other tourists on my way back up and enjoyed a laugh or two with them, not feeling in the least embarrassed. (Well, maybe a little, but happy to laugh at myself just the same.) A lovely Scotsman manning a food caravan let me into some nearby facilities for a wash-up, after which I treated myself to a black pudding burger and a lovely chat. Even though the castle was closed, I still had an adventure.

Stop and smell the flowers in **everything** you do. Get your hands dirty, slip in the mud, and for heaven's sake look up from your phone! You will not have a sense of living your purpose if your goal is just to get to the end of everything.

A while ago, a client was feeling utterly beleaguered by everything she needed to do to promote her work when what she really wanted to be doing was the work itself. She was in danger of burning out, something she'd done before, so it was a very challenging turning point for her. We talked about the minimum she could do that wouldn't overextend her, would still provide a positive return, and that would allow her to return to actually doing her work, both without regret and without exhaustion. Like most critical life decisions, once made the relief was palpable and she cried with the liberation from it. This is a very common exchange with creative, passionate people, especially those in helping services like coaching.

This is a typical point we come to when our soul is crying out for one thing and our head is telling us we have to go in a different direction. The tug-o-war between these parts of ourselves is exhausting and it will burn you out, physically, mentally and emotionally. Every part of us is happier when we let our soul take the lead. There may not be the same achievement that way, or perhaps not in the way we'd intended, but there is no achievement anyway if we've totally knocked ourselves out and life is miserable.

My client couldn't hear the voice of her soul; what she felt was extreme reluctance to do what she thought she was supposed to do. Every time she started some aspect of the marketing work, she felt tired and negative. She was busy trying to summon up her own energy all the time, not managing it and then beating herself up for it. She felt very emotional and she thought of herself as pathetic. Even when she did manage to do some of this work, the outputs and outcomes were tainted and poor, and things seemed to refuse to come together the way she wanted. As soon as I pointed out she was operating out of sync with her own authentic self – ie. her soul – she knew immediately the truth of what I was saying and was able to begin listening to her true self for direction. After that the decisions happened quickly and easily; she found a more balanced approach and went back to her real work.

You won't wake up every morning with all the answers.

Knowing your purpose doesn't mean you know it every day. I don't wake up every morning anticipating exactly what I'll be doing, where, how, and with whom. Nor do I wake up needing to know that either. My life flows and I allow it to. People and events weave in and out and I'm open to them and accept them easily. For the most part I feel that I'm within a flow, and I don't need to know precisely what comes next. Nor do I particularly analyse where I am in that flow – I don't feel I have to tick off any kind of markers along the way. I never think *okay, I'm at this point now and next it'll be that point.* I am where I am. I'm not completing a puzzle or sitting a test. Everything is as it should be and I just am.

My life is simultaneously both clear and simple, and very full. Knowing and living your purpose doesn't mean everything is clear all the time. I still occasionally have moments of confusion, where things may not be clear at all. I used to find these so annoying and frustrating; they'd often come right when I felt everything was so clear and on track, and I'd end up questioning whether it was right at all. This happened umpteen times before I came to understand that the fogginess and doubt were a part of the path and it was better if I just let the fog invade my space because it would soon leave just as quickly as it had come. Almost always the fog would give way to even greater clarity, so eventually I saw it as *essential* to the process of clarification. Like jumping into a really clear river or swimming hole – when you first dive in and swim around you'll muddy the water – it's a natural consequence of taking a leap into a new space. It's as though the Universe responds to your commitment to your purpose path with a flurry of supportive energy swirling around you in a sort of dust storm – it feels hazy but it eventually settles and things are even clearer than before. If you fight it though, you maintain the dust storm. Let it be and let it settle. You'll be surprised. There is absolutely no value whatsoever in responding to any lack of clarity with self-pity or whining – that amounts to fighting it and not only will it not help, it'll make it worse and it'll last longer.

Summary

Here's a summary of what purpose *isn't*:

- It's not simply about a job or a career; it's much broader and fuller than that.
- It's not an equation – there are no absolute elements to your purpose, and finding *your* purpose will be a different journey, with different emphases, from anyone else.
- It's not limited. It's not a place you get to and then you're there. It's never-ending journey that will last your whole life.
- It's not a magical mystery. Most of what you need to get on your purpose path you know already.

- It's not unknown to you. As you travel your purpose path, it will feel increasingly familiar.
- It's not tied to achievement. There are no boxes to tick on your purpose path, to say you got to a certain point.
- It won't always be clear. Periods of fogginess are a part of the process; don't fight them – embrace them.

2. The desire to know

More and more people are finding that the desire to know and live their purpose is a very powerful one. It's almost visceral and it can feel as though it's calling from deep inside ourselves.

It's a call to spirit. And it's a call *of* Spirit. It's a call from our true Self, and it's calling us *to* that Self, to discover our authentic core.

Living our purpose is the outward manifestation of our mature Spiritual Self.

We have many parts to our individual selves. Our Spiritual Self is one of those parts, just as we have an emotional self, an intellectual self, a sexual self, an aesthetic self, and so on. Living our purpose is the outward manifestation of our mature Spiritual Self.

Having rewarding, healthy relationships could be considered one manifestation of our best *emotional* Self – there could be several others: happiness, the ability to love and care for others. We have an *aesthetic* Self that needs art and music and theatre and beauty, and that part of our Self will be greater or lesser in all of us – if you're an artist then it's a big part of you.

We fulfil the needs of these parts in many varied ways. Our Spiritual Self looks for meaning, purpose, an understanding of why we are here and what the purpose of humanity is. Our Spiritual Self develops its own meaningful explanations of God, including whether we believe in a God of some kind or not, and if so, what God is.

None of these parts operate in isolation from each other. They stimulate and influence each other in a complex and often confusing, often rewarding, dance. We can even see how they can compete with each other. For example, one part of us is influenced by societal standards and norms, accepting some and rejecting others. Perhaps we could call this our *civic* Self. The societal expectation of having a career may thus compete with emotional and physical desires to live a happier, healthier life. Or we may find the expectation of having a career is in fact entirely congruous with a happier, healthier life. The balance we apply to our diverse desires will be different for all of us. No two of us is the same in the importance we place on the different parts of who we are, and the influence they have on us and the life choices we make. That's one of the particular beauties of our species.

We will experience distress though when parts of us go completely unnoticed or ignored or are out of sync with the value we give them. And this is truest of all when we ignore the call to purpose. How many times have we heard people say they achieved every business and financial success they could have imagined but yet they were miserable? It's a common story. This is the call to purpose happening. It's the desire for meaning, for meaningful work, and to make a contribution; to feel that we are doing something useful and that life itself has meaning. It is our Spirit calling. And nine times out of ten – ninety-nine times out of a hundred – that Spirit has been ignored, or very likely not even noticed. And it's waited patiently for us to fill up our lives with everything else we thought we wanted, knowing full well that its time would come. And then there it is, going *Hey! Over here!* happy as anything, joyful at the thought of finally being noticed, eager to help.

If we've had no input into this part of our Self at all, if the language of Spirit and Purpose has never been around us, then we may be in a really difficult position to move forward. We may be hearing a call to purpose, but we won't necessarily be hearing that as a spiritual pursuit. We might even be dead against the idea of it being anything to do with the spiritual.

Others of us with some kind of experience and initiation into the spiritual may start to go in this direction, but it's amazing how reluctant we can still be. My whole life has been one of spiritual seeker and yet I can see how slow I've been at times in giving attention to this critical part of my self.

Spirit loves to be wild!

Others of us with a few purpose-pursuing resources – courage being primary among them – will probably take the bull by the horns and do something radically different with our lives, and that's always a very, very good start in leading us towards our purpose path. Spirit loves to be wild.

The time is now!

Part of the urgency has to do with the idea of *now or never!* People feel they've perhaps left it too long, or they've been busy raising children or having a career, or both, and now it's *my time.*

We may start to worry about how much time is available to us, or more to the point how much really *useable, useful* time. Post-fifty we can be fairly confident half our life is over, and useful years remaining may be fewer than twenty, depending on our state of mind and physical well-being. And we all know how fast the previous twenty years flew by! This year I bought both my children vehicles but it doesn't seem that long ago I was still strapping them into their car seats!

Whilst it's important to get on with your purpose pursuit at whatever age you're hearing its call, there isn't quite the rush that you may feel. And once you are more firmly on your purpose route you will feel more content to be in the here and now rather than worrying about how much time has already passed you by and how little you may think is left.

I believe though that most of what you're feeling is the pull of your soul, waking you up, and saying *Time's up! My turn!* And you *must* answer that call. It will keep niggling at you, and not answering it will leave you increasingly frustrated. The change that has led you to this point where you're now thinking *What next?* or *This is my time now* was heard by your Soul and it's forced its way up through your over-thinking headspace and it's rearing to go.

And, what's more, it has **no concept at all of being too old** or too late or too unprepared. Time is irrelevant for Spirit. Except for that instant of time that is now.

Sixty is the new Twenty.

Turning sixty doesn't have to mean doing not-very-much anymore. In fact, there's no excuse for any such thing.

Fit and healthy sixty-somethings are just starting life over, selling up, going on adventures, starting new careers, going to live in exotic new places, going traveling, daring to do things they've dreamed of their whole lives and never thought they'd have the courage to do. Others who may be physically incapacitated in some way can also still have active and busy lives. As a nurse and caregiver in various roles I've seen too many people facing seemingly impossible hurdles and still managing to live full, flourishing lives, not to believe there are few excuses not to be living a purposeful life. I recently met a spectacular woman my age who lost a leg only a few years ago due to infection but soon after flew across a London stadium, hundreds of feet in the air on a trapeze at the Olympic opening ceremony. When I met her, she was heading off skiing with her new husband.

Today's sixty-pluses have particular advantages over those much younger, and certainly more than any previous generation's sixty-somethings.

Sixty-somethings (and mid to late fifty somethings) are the baby-boomers. We were born in an era of hope, we had some of the best education ever, we had more than our parents ever dreamed of having by a country mile, and **women baby-boomers** were the world's **main glass ceiling breakers** in every area of life. We're confident, we're resourced, we're knowledgeable, and we're **not interested in sitting back and watching the world go by** our window until we die.

We're the first generation to live exponentially longer than the one before us, and we're the first generation who really did indeed choose to *live*.

> At times, it seems to me
> that I am living my life backwards,
> and that at the approach of old age
> my real youth will begin.
>
> *André Gide*

Two generations ago, sixty was much older than it is now. Even one generation ago. My mother died way too young at forty-six and I'm now a decade older than her (a strange feeling, to be sure), but I'm still younger than her – in the way I dress, the way I behave, the activities I participate in, and much more. I'm fairly typical of my demographic, as she was of hers, but I'm fitter and, putting aside that she had cancer at an early age, I'm healthier. And I have a great deal more freedom to pursue my dreams and desires.

So don't ever wonder *is it too late?* because we are the generation for whom it's most certainly not! We can expect to be healthy into our nineties, if not further, and we can expect to have plenty that is meaningful and fulfilling as well.

And that doesn't just mean relishing grandparenthood, although it's a part of many of our lives at this point. There is a lot more adventure in you than running around with children again.

> ## I recently turned sixty.
> ## Practically a third of my life is over!
>
> *Woody Allen*

I'm not sure I'd be too keen to live to 180, but I am keen to make it to ninety fit and healthy, in which case I'm not yet two-thirds of the way there. And I'm quite sure these next thirty years or so are going to be as fulfilling, enlightening, exciting and soulful as the previous thirty, but in a whole different way. I'm freer to tune into my purpose now than I've been before, and that's probably the case for most of you. The reality of our second age – thirty to sixty – is that it *is* generally about career and marriage and children and creating a home and pursuing achievement, and all of that is our foundation for where we are now.

None of this means that life has been meaningless up to this point. We have all variously found satisfaction in our work and in being a parent and in learning mature emotional interaction. And there may have been a strong element of the spiritual in all of those things. If that's the case then you're very possibly several steps ahead on your purpose path than others for whom meaningfulness and spirituality haven't been a factor. Nonetheless, we are at the time we're at and the urge to meaning and spirit is louder than it's ever been before.

When this call begins, and comes slowly (or dramatically, as the case may be) into the foreground of our thinking, we can feel very lost. The question of what you're supposed to be doing, or what you even *want* to do, can be a complete mystery. Or if you have some clarity around the *what,* then the *how* is elusive. And so in the midst of this huge desire to **know**, our focus becomes very much on what we **don't know**. And then the strength of the desire *to* know, and the whole *don't know* thing can turn into a small fury of frustration and angst. It's almost like being a teenager all over again! All of the *Who am I?!* and *What do I want to do with my life?!* that were part of your youth can feel as though they're back with a vengeance.

Add a dash of scepticism, a pound of fear, and regular doses of beating ourselves up, and the desire to know may end up unheeded in a flurry of rationalising, and internal messages telling ourselves to *Grow up!*

There is only one solution, if old age is not to be an absurd parody of our former life, and that is to go on pursuing ends that give our existence a meaning.

Simone De Beauvoir

At this point you have three choices: *jump in, *forget about it (good luck with that), or *hang round on the edge procrastinating about jumping but not actually doing it. The worst you can do is the latter because you'll just be constantly beating yourself up over not jumping, or frustrated that the call to purpose won't go away but *what am I to do?* Really, you'll make yourself miserable. It's like being invited to a party and being made to wait in the corner. Who would do that? Most of us would either leave, or stay and try to enjoy ourselves regardless of what someone else says. Why on earth would you wait in the corner?! No sensible person would do that. And you're a sensible person. So, you know… you're either in or out. Right?

It doesn't matter at what age the call to purpose is heard, it has to be answered. If you're feeling the urge to dance, then dance. If you're hearing the call to paint, then paint. **Don't waste the probability that the Universe will step up to support you as soon as you take action.**

We've learnt through our adult lives that the mature person doesn't simply respond to impulses; that we need to apply our rational brain to think about what we're doing. The older I get, the more I'm in fact inclined to follow impulses, albeit within a fairly powerful set of boundaries (mostly to do with my values), and somewhat regardless of risk or perceived possibility. What I also find is that the impulses that come – or more to the point the opportunities that present themselves – tend increasingly to be precisely what I'd been thinking about doing anyway. Case in point: I've wanted to visit Greece – it's been on my list for a long time. And I've also wanted to plan a retreat. Late last year I was invited, totally out of the blue, by an almost complete stranger, to co-host a women's retreat in Greece. On top of that, one of my best friends then decided to come on the retreat too. That kind of thing happens more and more. And usually I can't say yes quickly enough.

Curiosity.

It is fundamentally human to be curious. It sets us apart as a species. Only we wonder at our own existence and ask *Why? Why am I here? Where did I come from? Where am I going?* These are the three fundamental questions of existence as a human being.

And yet, for so many millions of people – billions, even – the freedom to ask, and the right to answer, have been denied them by a society that is intent on control.

It is free societies that advance science and much of new thought, by fostering the curious. It is free societies that grow educational institutions. It is free societies that support every corner of the creative arts. Closed societies – theocracies, communist countries, dictatorships – limit freedom of thought and creativity and as a result can have a dearth of original arts and literature. The artist Ai Wei Wei in China and the writer Alexander Solzhenitsyn in Soviet Russia are two famous examples of dissenting artists in oppressive regimes. Against all odds though, both persisted both in their art and notably in their dissent, despite imprisonment for their views and work. They were, and are, rare though in their determination in face of such pressure.

A society doesn't have to be so overtly repressive though to limit our freedom to be curious. Societal pressure to conform exists throughout Western society to various degrees, restricting not by law but by the power to exclude, demean and disparage those who may choose to step outside a prescribed set of ideas and behaviours. The list of what has been scorned in the last fifty years alone is endless: punk, hippy culture, tattoos, modern art, every religion outside of Christianity, various types of Christianity, eating meat, not eating meat, being poor, having different coloured skin, voting liberal, voting conservative, voting green, voting at all, the car you drive, being rich, getting divorced, having short hair… we could all fill pages and pages with lists of what's been considered unacceptable to some group or another in our own societies in our own lifetimes.

It's no wonder then that we can find the idea of examining our own humanity and spirituality wrong, a weakness, something only *woowoo* people do, not to be taken seriously, embarrassing, silly, demonic, childish, irresponsible, and so on. Not to mention, in the face of so much pressure, frightening.

I have so many friends who've taken a massive turn in their career and intentions, away from the conventional and towards the less conventional, only to face scorn from family and friends. And this is very often in the context of a well-educated, fairly liberal and supposedly open demographic. *Are you still doing that writing thing?* Ouch!

Nonetheless, Spirit calls. Curiosity calls. Purpose calls.

Many years ago, I somewhere read the words: *If you don't let your creativity out, it will beat you bloody inside.* They're words I've never forgotten, and I've come to believe somewhat similarly of the call from Spirit. Spirit won't beat you up on the inside – any inside beating-up is entirely our own doing, but nor will it go away. And you can bet you will keep colliding up against challenges it sets before you to try to get you to listen.

Don't fear your curiosity. If there are questions inside you that are hungry for answers, go look for those answers. The search to know who you are and why you're here is the greatest adventure of life, and in its pursuit your curiosity is a gift. Indulge it. Humour it. Give it the time of day. Make room for it. Create space to foster it.

Purpose Self-assessment ©

Where you are at in your purpose journey only you can fully comprehend, but I've put together a small questionnaire (See Appendix I) that I hope will help you to assess that. I'm not keen on the idea of assessment, especially of something so subjective and personal as this, but I'm also aware that we are all susceptible to the thought that we've not got very far, or that we've got such a long way to go, and those thoughts can frustrate our journey before we feel we've even started.

It's divided into six sections: your spiritual life, your life generally, your work, your goals, your relationships, and your own general attitudes. It's aimed at giving you the simplest of ideas of where you're at and where the priority areas for attention might be.

Do these sections and your answers surprise you? Do you feel encouraged by where you're at? Where do you think you need to give more attention? Is there any section that's overwhelmingly underdeveloped? Which sections are well developed?
In a random survey conducted via my main author Facebook page and my email list, from 300 respondents, the average score was 106/150. The lowest score was 6, and the highest was 150.

The highest scoring statements were:

- I believe in something bigger than myself (Q1)
- I like to help others (Q7)
- I'm grateful for what I have in my life (Q25)

The lowest scoring statements were:

- My work offers me opportunities for learning and growth, without too much stress (Q15)
- I work on my goals consistently (Q19)

Summary

So, in summary, this call to purpose that you're experiencing:

- It's a call *of* Spirit, and *to* Spirit.
- If it's ignored, it will cause distress.
- Like many others, you're feeling this call *now;* it probably has a sense of urgency about it.
- Far from being too old, you're at a brilliant time of life to be pursuing your purpose.
- Your natural curiosity is a great tool in the pursuit of your purpose. Allow it to flourish.

3. Distractions

There is a myriad of ways we get in our own way, almost all of them the result of giving our thoughts more attention and more authority than they deserve. We tend to think of our thoughts as our own, that they're the real us and that we need to listen to them and explore them. As we get to know our thoughts and thought patterns better we begin to realise this is an illusion. For the unfolding of our purpose, and just to be happier, we need to learn to ignore a lot of our thoughts. They are the language of ego, and we need to listen more to the language of our soul.

Ego is the counterweight to your Soul.

There are many understandings of the ego. I don't mean ego as in egotism (ie. egotistical), or in egoism (conceit). I don't especially mean ego as in Freud's construction of the psyche (id, ego & super-ego), which is very complex, although insofar as Freud combines aspects of our **conscious intention** with **unconscious instincts** to form *the main driver* of our everyday life and behaviour, there is some truth in his views.

Ego is based firmly in the mind. **It is that part of us that responds defensively, to whatever it sees as a threat to our sense of ourselves.** Ego believes its job is to protect us, but in so doing it limits our experience and our opportunity to try new things.

Ego blocks personal growth.

Sometimes this is a good thing, sometimes it gets us in trouble. Other times **it totally blocks the desire for personal change and growth,** something it tends to view with great fear.

Our ego provides for our personal protection and motivation in so many ways. Ego gives us ambition, confidence, and self-assertion. And these are all very useful to have. **But try to face your own weaknesses or take a look at parts of yourself you don't like, or let go the mind in order to commune with the spirit, and ego will hold on tight.** It doesn't want us to feel humiliated or out of control – that's its job, but sometimes we need to gently and lovingly put it aside.

- The ego sees itself as separate from everything and everyone – it's very individualistic.
- The soul understands that it is part of a great whole, both unique in its own part and one with the whole at the same time.
- The ego sees only itself. It believes itself to be real and the soul to not be real.
- The soul *knows* itself to be real and the ego to not be real.

A wise person denies ego at their peril. At advanced stages of spiritual development, we may turn to the goal of full release of the ego – but for those of us living in the world, *mindfulness* of ego during one's purpose journey is more than sufficient. Ego is not your enemy; it's more a somewhat poor-thinking (or indeed over-thinking) and stubborn child that needs love and reassurance to feel safe in the presence of the soul.

> The most strongly enforced of all known taboos is the taboo against knowing who or what you really are behind the mask of your apparently separate, independent, and isolated ego.
>
> *Alan Watts*
> *The Book on the Taboo Against Knowing Who You Are*

You have to let go of some of who you think you are.

Letting go of anything we've grown attached to – people, things, our beliefs and our view of the world, the person we think we are – is always a challenge.

For some reason, we never expect to have to let go of anything, which is pretty silly when you think about it since life is constantly throwing up things we have to let go of. It would be far more useful if we realised this sooner rather than later and learnt how to do it. Like everything else, we get better at it the more we have to deal with it. And the more we resist ever letting go, the harder it is. You will inevitably *have* to let go of some things you may have held onto for years, in order simply to survive. And that is a whole lot harder.

One of the things we least realise we need to let go of is who we think we are. If your dreams are all about traveling the world, you need to give up being where you are now. You probably need to give up the idea of being poor (which, by the way, doesn't mean you have to be rich), and you may need to give up the idea of having a house, and having a normal job, and a whole bunch of other things. You almost certainly need to give up the idea that you're someone who doesn't succeed at making her dreams come true.

If you look back on your life and all you can see are your mistakes and failures, you're going to have to not only let go of this view of yourself but write a different story about your life – one that describes all your many successes and joys – because that is the foundation you will need to truly grow into your purpose.

Letting go helps us to live in a more peaceful state of mind
and helps restore our balance.
It allows others to be responsible for themselves,
and for us to take our hands off situations that do not
belong to us. It frees us from unnecessary stress.

Melody Beattie

Depth not Breadth.

A fatal error for the ardent pursuer of purpose is to keep trying lots of different things, in the hope that one of those things will leap out at you as the answer to all your purpose prayers.

This doesn't work. It can't. This is the scattergun approach to trying to find your purpose. Not only is it shallow, but the notion that we're acquiring meaning is an illusion. We may well be acquiring lots of interesting skills that in the moment feel great, but as long as you're grazing superficially across many potential opportunities, you're not going deep into any one thing, and therefore you're not really acquiring true meaning.

Course junkies do this. I've had a number of clients and friends who are course junkies. They love learning and trying new things, and I totally get that. I love it too. But it would also totally do my head in. And what I see with those who do this, is that they become so increasingly committed to this mode of pursuit that they can't stop and they lack the ability to stick with anything, because it doesn't feel like the absolutely perfect thing. They miss out on the very real and life-changing challenges that come from sticking with something and going deep into it and facing up to whatever parts of ourselves we rub up against when we do that.

True pursuit of purpose is not achieved via grazing. You have to sit down to a proper meal, at the table, and take your time with what's in front of you.

Don't make the work you're doing now a distraction.

There's value in every new experience, good or bad. A job may feel like it's dead-end or unfulfilling but even those feelings are potentially clues to learning opportunities.

You will almost certainly find, when you do get to a point where you feel you're in your purpose, that there's been a point and a value to everything you've done prior to that.

The point to mentioning this is two-fold:
1) There's not a lot of value in being gloomy about what you're doing now. If you've got a whole lot of negative feelings about your current situation, you're just adding more obstacles.
2) It may well be that you need to move on from that situation, but don't be in a rush to do so before you've got what you came for. Maybe you can't get on with your boss? Honestly, how much of that is about you? How can you learn to get on with her anyway? There will be a way. If someone difficult is in front of you, they may well be there to teach you something about yourself. Of course, it might be that what you're supposed to learn is to get the hell out of there, but that's not always what

it's about. I can promise you if you don't learn from the situation, it'll come up again.

I've had so many different life and work experiences, many I never planned to have, others I never dreamed I'd have; I learned from all of them, even the deadbeat ones, and especially the really challenging ones that I really wanted to run a mile from. Ask yourself the question often: *What is this situation trying to teach me?* Be honest and learn those lessons.

> Learn the lesson of your own pain.
> Learn to seek God, not in any single event of past history, but in your own soul, in the constant verifications of experience.
> *Mary Augusta Ward*

I've had several key turning points in my life, including things as dire as my mother's death when I was just twenty years old. In my working life, an important change occurred as a result of a period of a few years when I had two wonderful jobs but where I was working with a host of deceitful, grossly narcissistic personalities; *and* I was in a romantic relationship with a deceitful, grossly narcissistic personality at the same time. That was several years ago and I'm still occasionally learning from it. Many of you will have had relationships – professional, family, partner – with narcissistic personalities. We do indeed need to run from them, but not before you figure out what it is that allows you to be attracted to them in the first place. It's a little challenging when it's family (a parent, say), but when it's a romantic relationship especially, it's almost always due to some lack of self-esteem on your part. I don't want to have a discussion here about narcissism – there are plenty of resources around now on that topic – but they are extremely challenging relationships from which we can learn an enormous amount about ourselves. And you *must* learn those lessons or you will be pulled back into the next narcissistic web that comes your way, without any shadow of doubt.

Don't indulge yourself.

We all need to discern better and worse ways of giving ourselves treats.

> When we don't get any treats, we feel depleted, resentful, and angry, and we feel justified in self-indulgence. We start to crave comfort – and grab that comfort wherever we can, even if it means breaking good habits.
>
> *Gretchen Rubin*

Food and alcohol binges are not a treat. (By which you should not assume I never do these things, because I do, because I'm flawed. But I do them increasingly less.)

Bad treats, that may provide short-term hedonistic pleasure with medium-term unpleasantness and *dis-ease* and no long-term advantage at all, also include:

- Recreational drug use
- Binge television
- Staying up all night (partying, binge television, etc)
- Retail therapy (not always)
- Doing nothing all day (although occasionally essential)
- You can think of more, I know

Good treats, that may or may not always provide short-term gains, but will provide medium and long-term ones, include:

- Exercise, regularly and especially in nature
- Growing things
- Cleaning up – it's always wonderful to relax in a clean, tidy space
- Reading something inspirational for an hour or two
- You can think of more of these too…

The whole concept of treats has become ridiculous. When I was a kid, roast chicken on Sunday was a treat; now I can have it every day if I want to. Presents came twice a year on birthdays and Christmas; now I can buy myself presents any time. I can eat chocolate every day, watch a movie every day, do nothing all day for *several* days or even weeks.

They're no longer treats.

Of course, our lives are more privileged now and some things rightfully become everyday things. But *everything?* Many such things deserve to remain occasional.

> In a nation that was proud of hard work,
> too many of us now tend to worship
> self-indulgence and consumption.
> *Jimmy Carter*

The reduction of treats doesn't have to be nun-like – this isn't about denying ourselves every enjoyable thing. It does mean being more mindful of how much we indulge ourselves as a distraction from doing or facing some other thing that we need to do or face.

Dichotomies & Contradictions.

We live in a world loaded with dichotomies and contradictions, which seemingly most people don't recognise, because most of the time we want answers, we want them now, and we try to see our world in terms that are black and white, good and bad, left and right, when the truth is either in the middle and/or encapsulates both the black *and* the white.

> ## Contradiction is not a sign of falsity,
> ## nor the lack of contradiction a sign of truth.
>
> *Blaise Pascal*

In any given situation, there might in reality be two or more right answers. The problem arises when either 1) we dogmatically assert one of those answers, completely denying the value of any other, or 2) we do indeed see two or more right answers, recognising that they are also opposite in some way, and we can struggle with living within this dichotomy. The latter manifests at a higher evolutionary level where the individual takes an appropriately broader and more considered view of the world but that individual is equally, if not more, confused than the former who can be entirely happy with his singular, perhaps blinkered, view.

> ## I believe that truth has only one face:
> ## that of a violent contradiction.
>
> *Georges Bataille*

Here are some examples:

- I want to give my children freedom of choice but I also want to give them boundaries. Where do I draw the line? Can a line even be drawn?
- I want to love and forgive unconditionally but I'm not going to tolerate certain behaviours.
- I want stability but I want adventure.
- How to stay highly present and live in the moment, but simultaneously set goals for the future.
- How to be rational and thoughtful but not over-think.
- Knowing what you want but also remaining open to other possibilities.
- To be grateful for what you have but still want more.
- To accept my family and friends for who and what they are *and* to help them believe they can be and have more.
- To be realistic about what's wrong in the world at the same time as not giving it undue and stress-inducing attention.
- To take responsibility for past actions, without taking on guilt.
- I have to work hard to get what I want, but if I believe in God/the Universe, then shouldn't I expect it all to come to me regardless.

This is real life. And it is real maturity to be able to hold apparently contradictory notions in your mind at the same time. And to be okay with that, rather than to be troubled by it.

For the spiritual seeker, it is at the nexus of these conflicts that we can find our most significant opportunities for personal growth, as we first recognise the basis on which we form our different and opposing views and how we feel about them. We are influenced in our points of view by government, society, the media, the common view, our emotions and our higher spiritual perspectives. From each of these perspectives our views on any given topic will rub up against each other and may cause us discomfort. Here is where we explore ourselves, our behaviour, our beliefs, and most of all how we can rise up to a higher version of ourselves. It's never easy work, but it's worth doing.

> **Only by learning to live in harmony with your contradictions can you keep it all afloat.**
>
> *Audre Lorde*

Do What You Have to Do.

And be happy about it!

Every one of us has to do things we'd rather not – the necessities of life: cooking, cleaning, mowing the lawns, maybe a job that we're not keen on right now, but we all still have to pay the bills.

Sometimes, even when our purpose is clear, we have to do other things along the way. In fact, we've *been* doing other things along the way up until now. Every one of those things forms part of our purpose and our journey, and every one of them teaches us something.

In every religious tradition in the world, initiates have had to involve in the daily routine; sometimes that's all they do for years. Monks have gardened, cleaned floors, tended animals… There is an important type of spiritual connectedness that goes with being happy with having to do the most mundane things. One of my most frequent pieces of advice to people I work with is if you're feeling unhappy, go clean! I don't know what it is about cleaning, but it's satisfying and somehow gets us out of ourselves in some way.

There is a balancing act in the pursuit of your purpose between doing what you have to do and saying *Enough!* and taking a leap of faith into something new. I advocate both. (Even then there will always still be things you *have* to do.) Only you can know when the time is right to launch yourself into something new.

There's also a balancing act between learning to live purposefully regardless of what you're doing and finding the particular purpose you want to live. We also need to be able to do both of these. Living your purpose has a lot more to it than finding that one thing that you believe will make you happy and purposeful; you can choose to live life purposefully now, with all that that means. In fact, the more purposefully you *live* the more likely you are to find your purpose. This is a little of the beautiful poetry of purpose.

And as you've hopefully seen, what I've just said, in the two paragraphs above, holds both a bunch of contradictions and an enormous amount of wisdom. Do ponder on these. Contradiction is natural to life – life is rarely 'either/or'.

Don't think that what you have to do now is a distraction, because as soon as you think it's a distraction it does indeed become one.

Let go the past and the future.

Letting go the past – it can take a while to let go events and feelings that have a grip on us from the past: old hurts, trauma, relationships... Generally, they're holding on to us because there are still things we need to learn about ourselves as a result of them, much of which will be about our self-worth. A good coach will help you work through these things pretty efficiently.

Letting go the future – this is a different kettle of fish. The mistake we make about the future is that we put off being happy until then. We think we'll just do such-and-such and then we'll be happy. We'll just do that thing, achieve something else, and then we'll be happy. Happiness doesn't work like that. If you can't be happy without that thing, you can't be happy. Happiness is not thing-based. It's now-based.

Nothing holds you back from your future more than the past. We all have a past, but some people's pasts have their claws into them and won't let go; other people are so attached to the past that they hold on and hold on and hold on, hoping to re-live their glory days. It never, ever works like that.

You absolutely cannot create the future you want for yourself as long as you're stuck in that old relationship, still angry at your parents, still seething over that old boss, still grieving for a loss.

Any one of those things could be 'justified' – I'm not saying you don't have a right to be angry, but how long are you going to keep holding onto damaging anger? How long are you going to let someone keep breaking your heart every day? How long will your sadness block your way to living your life? You cannot go back and change any of it. None of us are going that way. You can choose to stay stuck thinking how you might do that though. Or you can let it go and move on. Those are your choices. Simple.
Letting go isn't always easy. You need to work on it every day and eventually the pain and the attachment subside.

Regret and shame are two very strong emotions that hold us in the past. Neither has any value. This isn't to say that we shouldn't acknowledge past mistakes – in fact it's vital that we do acknowledge them as that's also how we move on. We've somehow acquired a foolish belief that to have a conscience and be responsible means we have to forever carry around our past with us and keep on apologising for it forever and a day. This just isn't so. You can separate the requirement to be a responsible adult from having to carry guilt, shame and regret with you forever. The former is important, the latter not in the least.

Don't spend too much time looking into the past. Learn what you can and then move on. It doesn't matter what you've done. You can't go back and change any of it. You *can* learn, which is a large part of why we're here. Maybe you can apologise to some people. You can certainly forgive yourself. And you can have on hand the knowledge you'll need for the future. But beyond that, there's no reason to spending time in your head back then.

I could write several books about all the mistakes I've made in my life. I could write several more on what I've learnt from them. We all could. Sometimes it can take us years – decades even – to move on from past events. Some hurts will do that. But if you're struggling to move on from the shitty boss you had five years ago, or the marriage that ended ten years ago, then you need to get some help to let go, because you're just harming yourself at this point.

You must live your life *now*. Living your life back then is an utter waste of a life, of your talents, of everything you've been given and that's available to you to live now and make a contribution now and be happy and fulfilled now. Don't do that to yourself. It will be a major regret in your life, and then the regret of it will be the next thing you'll have to let go of and move on from.

The death of a loved one is one of the hardest things to move on from, and indeed for a while we quite naturally don't. We think about our memories with that person, maybe what we could have said, hopefully thankful for all that we had with them. Sometimes our love for them seems accompanied by a feeling of guilt if we move on with our own lives; although I think most of us know, when we think about it, that's not what our dear departed would wish for us. Sometimes our pain continues on into a clinical depression, and at that point we must seek help.

Moving on doesn't mean the past doesn't have value. It's just that you don't live there now.

Stop whining.

I like to distinguish a little between whining and complaining. They're both pretty bad, but whining has a quality about it that makes you wince a little and feels like someone's scratching their fingernails down a blackboard. It's a type of complaining that has little or no substance or possibly even truth to it and is much more an indication of the personality of the person doing the whining. It's very unattractive and so for that reason alone it's not worth doing. But more importantly, *any* negative expression acts like a brick wall around your Spirit and prevents the flow of all things positive in your life.

Then there's the distinction between complaining and complaining: complaining that is about expressing your dissatisfaction only – also known as *bitching*; and complaining that is about expressing concern with a desire for solutions and action and change. The latter is acceptable complaining as long as it's about identification of things that need fixing rather than simply bemoaning them; the former is only a small step above whining.

You cannot be in a position to receive love if you're giving out hate. Likewise, if you're spewing negativity then you're not able to receive anything that's positive. One of the keys to being able to know our purpose is via the insights that come to us when we're living positively. No one ever received any inspirational insight when they were expressing what's wrong with the world and everything and everyone in it, and frequent complaining and whining keeps you in a state that is invisible to the Universe's inspiration and connection.

When you feel the urge to complain, practise stopping yourself. It's not easy and it takes time – years even – to learn to reverse this bad habit. Somehow in the culture of the last few decades of learning to express our feelings, we've really gone overboard and we've become a very negative culture as a result. We even feel we have a *right* to our complaints. When you feel a complaint coming on, immediately switch your thinking to something positive and good. This doesn't mean you shouldn't pay attention to what's wrong in the world – I'm not talking about burying your head in the sand. I believe we should be aware of what's going on in the world, politically, socially, etc. But we don't have to add our own negativity to what's already so negative. Either think about what you can do to make a difference, or transform your own negative energies to positive ones, since that after all *is* making a difference in the world.

De-clutter

These days this doesn't need much introduction. We're all realising that a) we've acquired too much stuff, and b) that it can sit like an albatross around our necks. Few of us are going to start baking up a storm in a messy kitchen. We need to start with everything clean and tidy and in its place. For most of us it's the same with our desk.

I had a client once that had a sign on her office door that said *A tidy desk is the sign of a sick mind.* But honestly the woman never got a thing done. Nor could she find anything. She basically just didn't want to change. She was lovely. A wonderful, kind, welcoming person. But nothing ever happened. Possibly it wouldn't have happened even with a clean desk, but the thing is she was wedded to her clutter. She would have needed to have insight into how it acted as an obstacle before she was willing to change it.

Creating order is very reassuring.

My son was a stand-up comedian for two and a half years after he left high school. His entire being was taken up with finding the next funny story or joke. As a teenager he always had a typically messy bedroom. He left me speechless the day he mentioned that tidying his room up helped him think and write better. As though I'd never mentioned it. I'm waiting for the day he tells me meditating helps him think and write better too, 'cos I've never mentioned that before either. He's now a very busy chef at a top restaurant and his life is very intense. No one knows the importance of a clean work space like a chef and I'm sure that aspect of his work carries into all manner of other parts of his life now too.

Fair warning: de-cluttering can be a great procrastination tool as well. Especially for writers. I had to go write in a café when I was writing fiction or I'd tidy my house to within an inch of its life.

When our life holds a lot of 'stuff', we can more easily get caught up in it and forget the stuff we're really here for. The same is true when we have a lot of emotional clutter, and a good clean-out can include releasing some of that kind of 'stuff' too.

I've spent years de-cluttering. I started after I'd moved a huge house load from one end of the country to the other twenty years ago, and came to open one of those really large, metre-high packing boxes only to discover it was full of glass jars. Empty ones. And I don't preserve or make jam. It was truly an *Oh my god!* moment. Now, twenty years on, I've de-cluttered so much and am now on an extended travel period, with a small storage unit in my hometown, a few boxes of seasonal clothes at various friends' homes around the world, and everything else in my suitcase. It's bliss!

4. The elements of purpose – a recap

A recap from my first book about the elements of purpose.

You have a purpose.

Of course, you do.

Proving it to yourself, if that's what you need, will be your own individual pursuit. And it will undoubtedly be a spiritual one rather than an intellectual one.

It's a bit like when people ask me why I believe in God, to which I say, I don't *believe* in God; I *know* God. I have *experienced* God, so I don't need to believe, because I know. So, you have a purpose. I know.

Everyone has a purpose.

But just for argument's sake, if it's not true that you have a purpose, well, what would be the point of living with that belief anyway? We are all happier when we're living purposefully. And when we're happier and living our purpose, we're also a lot healthier, our relationships are more fulfilling, and we're generally more successful too.

You have a soul, a spiritual Self. Your purpose and your spiritual Self go together. And your soul knows what your purpose is. Connecting with the one connects you with the other.

Individuals' own religious and spiritual beliefs will variously explain the origins of both us and our purpose and I urge you to read widely to grow and develop your own views on this. The breadth and diversity of religion and philosophy in this regard mostly proves to me that we simply cannot have full knowledge of such things. We will all have different experiences; indeed, everyone's purpose is their own unique purpose. And how beautiful is that?! There are seven-point-something billion views about the spiritual world and seven-point-something different purposes as well.

> **Believe in your heart**
> **that you're meant to live a life**
> **full of passion, purpose,**
> **magic and miracles.**
>
> *Roy T. Bennett*
> *The Light in the Heart*

Your purpose is your passion.

It is true that to do what we love is a huge key to living our purpose. But be really clear: watching television all day – even reading books all day – is not it. There are a lot of things we love to do that are just indulgences. Some indulgences are healthier than others but they are mostly still indulgences. Of course, there are a few people who've made reading books all day into a career and good for them, but that's not most of us.

So, if your passions are limited to Netflix, Facebook, eating chocolate and drinking wine… you need some new passions. Because these are almost certainly not going to take you in the direction of living your purpose; they're simply distractions.

Speaking as a Netflix and social media addict myself, I know I have to limit these as much as possible or I lose sight of what I'm really all about. And considering I run several Facebook pages and several Facebook groups, I really have to watch myself.

It's very possible that the thing you love doing, the thing that may be a significant aspect of your purpose, is something you're not actually doing very much. Maybe it's the thing you're going to do *one day*, when you have time, when you've got your life together, when you can afford to do it. There is a long list of excuses people have that are obstacles to doing what they love.

Stop that kind of thinking and start doing the 'one day' thing now. Because unless you are doing that thing, you're not going to be able to create a life that revolves around doing that thing. The way to create that life is by doing that thing *now*.

You don't have to be doing it in some great big way. Maybe you've still got your day job, and maybe you need to keep your day job because there are mouths to feed and bills to pay – I really get all that. But if you want to be a writer, then you need to write every day. If you want to make and sell home-made pies, then you need to be making a batch of your pies on the weekend and selling them. If you want to be a lawyer, then you can start a night school class. I could go on and on…

What is passion?
It is surely the becoming of a person.
Are we not, for most of our lives, marking time?
Most of our being is at rest, unlived.
The more expressed one's passion is, the more unbearable does life seem without it.

John Boorman
Projections

Your changing Purpose.

Purpose is a flow, a rhythm. It goes different places, changes course, goes fast sometimes, slow others.

It is absolutely not the case, and never has been, that we're supposed to get to some place in our lives and stay there.

There are a bunch of things to know about this.

One is that just when you thought you knew really clearly where you were going, often you can suddenly feel terribly foggy and indecisive about it, and then you can easily start to doubt whether you had nailed it or not.

A lot of my clients have this experience. Actually, all of them at some point. They'll say *I thought I had it, and now it doesn't feel like that was it at all.*

If you felt good about where you were headed, that foggy feeling now doesn't mean what you were feeling before was wrong. In my experience, episodes of clarity and vision can often be followed by cloudy periods. It's as though the new action you've taken around your purpose has drummed up a dust storm around you, and as far as I can tell, not only does this pass, it's also a good thing and usually leads to even greater clarity.

Two, sometimes things can feel like they're going so fast that you've got the speed wobbles. Other times it feels like nothing's happening. All of that is fine; it's not always going to be fast-paced and exciting. If you're taking action, then something's always happening, even if you don't see it yourself. Within limits, try to go with the flow. Follow your intuition.

> ## Change is not made without inconvenience, even from worse to better.
>
> *Richard Hooker*

Three, you will have various purposes in your life. There will be large over-riding ones at different times, especially if one of them is being a parent – parenting tends to dominate for a while, and fair enough. The end of the main period of parenthood can bring a massive vacuum for many women, marked as much by loss as by the need to find a new purpose.

The world is changing rapidly. You and your purpose will be moved by those changes too; your purpose is not static, nor is it uninfluenced by the world we live in. One of my clients lived near the terrifying apartment block fire in London in 2017 and she described a huge pall over her purpose and life for days. That kind of feeling doesn't mean that anything is wrong with you or that you have to change anything; no woman is an island and we are all affected by what goes on around us.

> Change always involves a dark night
> when everything falls apart.
> Yet if this period of dissolution

Your Unchanging Purpose.

I believe as human beings we have a fundamental intention and purpose in being here, which is to develop ourselves *as* human beings, by which I mean to develop those qualities and characteristics that make us human. These are the virtues, of which there are many, including: love, courage, kindness, mindfulness, trust, wisdom, forgiveness, justice, service, etc.

I believe we all have this purpose, first and foremost. And it is certainly upon the development of these that other aspects of our purpose are either revealed, built or enabled. Let me give you some examples.

Courage is the basis of all change. Most of us are more comfortable not changing, which if you want to find and live your purpose is going to be a bit of a drag, in the motoring sense of the word: without courage, you will be held back.

It's frequently the case that in the pursuit of your purpose you have to take some faith-filled, running jumps, which may or may not have soft landings. If you want to change your life in even a moderate way, you'll need courage.

Another example: if you are stuck in not **forgiving**, and if something from your past is hanging around and occupying too much of your heart and mind, this will be a block to your purpose, and often a very large one. **It prevents the flow of love** and thus the flow of spirit and the flow of purpose through your life, big time.

Courtesy, kindness and trust are wonderful enablers. You'll meet people, people will like you, and things will move in your direction if you're able to give of yourself in this way to others. This by no means spells 'doormat', okay? Wisdom teaches us tomato is a fruit but not to put it in a fruit salad. It also teaches us whom we trust and under what circumstances, but it doesn't put a wall up against trusting everyone.

Purpose has service as a defining characteristic.

Many, many people find their purpose in **service**. Not that they find it in a particular service necessarily (although they may), but that repeated and varied acts of service, in and of themselves, create some kind of profound generosity on the part of the Universe, of

Life, of God, in reflecting back to us in the form of connection to Spirit and to our purpose.

> The purpose of human life is to serve,
> and to show compassion
> and the will to help others.
>
> *Albert Schweitzer*

The growth of virtues doesn't imply piety and prudery; this is not a lesson in narrow-minded, medieval or Victorian morals. Learning the virtues is not a practice in applying blinkers to one's vision but rather in broadening your vision in the exploration of what it means to love, to forgive, to serve; of the depths and meaning of truth and compassion. The virtues are a vast tool in the pursuit of our purpose, and just one of them has the strength to carry us in the direction of our purpose.

There will be obstacles. They are lessons.

You will hit road blocks. (Or at least that's what they'll feel like.)

Life is a game though and not to be taken at all seriously.

Well, in one way. When kids play, they'll play one game for ages, but then they'll just as quickly stop and they often won't know what to play next. And sometimes there'll even be squabbles during that period, till they find their play rhythm again.

Finding and living your purpose operates in a similar way. It works really well when we're on a roll and in the groove and it almost feels like playing, but from time to time the rhythm of the game changes and we have a period of discomfort till we get back into the game again.

Road blocks can include our own emotional limitations and behaviour, changes in your life circumstances, or (what seems to be) other people putting up road blocks of some kind.

Never think your purpose is lost, or that this really is some kind of block, or even a mis-step. It's generally not. If you had that whole flow thing going on before, then you'll get it again, as long as you remember that it's a fun game. If you get too serious then you will stuff up the flow. The Universe does not like us being serious; it wants to play.

If you've been feeling like things are going along great and you suddenly feel completely unclear (and you *will* get those moments), don't worry! Worrying is the worst thing you can do. **Trust the Universe.** I know that sounds like a cliché, and well… it is; but, it's also true. It's true in the situation of having been on a roll, in your groove, feeling confident about direction. If a lack of clarity seems to rise up in the midst of that, then the Universe is just preparing for a better, more fun game, and it's likely that something new and exciting will pop up soon to take you even further along your purpose path.

Everyone has obstacles in the way of finding and living their purpose.

Everyone. We've built them up over a lifetime and we can't unbuild them overnight. Yet oddly we expect to delete them quickly. It's rare that it happens that way.

Don't beat yourself up for having created obstacles in your own way – we've all done it, and anyway beating yourself up is one of the obstacles, so you'll need to stop that too.

Don't think you can stop beating yourself up overnight. And don't beat yourself up for how long it takes to stop beating yourself up.

Every bit of self-awareness work you do on yourself will chip away at your obstacles and bring you closer to your purpose. And it's not just that you get closer because you've knocked a bit of wall down; you get closer because you've expanded your awareness and tuned in more to who you really are.

> Only in growth, reform, and change, paradoxically,
> is true security to be found.
>
> *Anne Morrow Lindbergh*
> *The Wave of the Future*

Almost every bit of obstacle removal is painful. It usually goes something like this. Some bit of ourselves that we probably don't like or we're very embarrassed to have gets pointed out to us by someone or something and we feel pretty shitty as a result. Very often we don't realise that we even have a problem to start with; often it feels like someone else has the problem. Some people will spend their whole lives blaming other people for their problems and never look inside themselves. Don't be one of those people.

> You will either step forward into growth,
> or you will step back into safety.
>
> *Abraham Maslow*

It often fills us with shame and embarrassment to find defects within ourselves, but, speaking from experience, if you're prepared to go the distance in revealing your faults and owning them, then shame melts away and you grow as a result. If you're a novice, then this is a process that requires a skilled coach or counsellor. If you've been down that road a lot, then you'll find the combination of a skilled friend and your own honesty can often be all you need.

> Growth is an erratic forward movement:
> two steps forward, one step back. Remember that
> and be very gentle with yourself.
>
> *Julia Cameron, The Artist's Way*

Help others with their purpose.

If you get the opportunity (and if you're a parent, you especially have that opportunity) have **the purpose conversation** with others. Frankly, have it with as many people as you can.

Here's how some of how that conversation could go:

Do you believe you have a purpose?
What do you think you're here for?
What would give more meaning to your life?
What do you think is in the way of you realising your purpose?
How much do your beliefs limit you? and *What are those beliefs?*
If you could do anything you wanted, what would that be?
What do you think it means to have a purpose? and *What do you think purpose is?*

It's of huge value to assist others with their purpose. In any way at all. You'll learn more about what purpose is all about (because as you'll be beginning to see it's not as simple as most people think when they first start pondering it).

> You can get everything in life you want if you will just help enough other people get what they want.
>
> *Zig Ziglar*

One enormous key to helping others with their purpose is to support them in their purpose-driven choices. Everyone's view of the world is different, and everyone's view of their own life is different. If someone's committed to finding and living their purpose, and they're taking action towards that, then supporting their decisions and choices is one of the best things you can do for them. You may not agree with what they're doing, but short of something terribly self-destructive, what you think generally doesn't matter, **at all**.

Being there for people, and holding a space for them and their purpose, is one of our greatest expressions of love.

Social Justice: Making a contribution.

Making a contribution is a key aspect of purpose. The world has to need what you have to offer, even if it doesn't know it yet.

The desire to make a difference is something I hear every day from most of the people I work with. Many are interested in engaging in some kind of social justice work, including aiding women, children, animals, the poor, veterans, and so on – some group that's being under-served by the community in some way.

There are many ways to make a contribution – in fact in some ways it's almost impossible not to. But in a world that's suffering and chaotic in a million different ways, there are groups everywhere for whom your input may be the difference even between life and death, or certainly between a life worth living and not.

It's a factor of the maturity of your heart and your soul that you are able to look around to see whose life you can assist, in the knowledge not only that you yourself have good fortune, but that you have something to offer.

That said, it's not always clear to us *how* we can make a difference, let alone what skills we have to offer. There's only so much soup kitchen volunteering most of us could do.

That said, you will find a world of inspiration in getting into the community and doing *some*thing. Getting started – from any particular point – is key to moving forward and finding the way.

There is no true purpose that doesn't also make a positive contribution to the world. By definition, if your contribution is negative, you're nowhere near your purpose.

I've spent the last few years travelling the world. That could very easily look entirely about me. But I know I made a contribution many places I went, with many people I spent time with. And I know also that I set an example to many other women just because I've had the courage to take on this slightly crazy, nomadic lifestyle; something I know others admire. Besides which I am able to work from wherever I am. And I believe that by living in joy I make a contribution also.

> Everyone must decide whether they will walk in the light of creative altruism or in the darkness of destructive selfishness.
>
> *Martin Luther King Jr.*

Making a contribution doesn't mean you're going to become the next Gandhi or Eleanor Roosevelt, although you could. Few of us will ever be that immortalised by the contributions we've made, but you can be sure that your contribution, alongside billions of others, will make a difference.

How is it that *making a difference* is an aspect of purpose? By definition somehow your purpose must be positive. Some people can sure seem purposeful about their very negative contributions, I know. But what is their purpose really? Money? Power? There is no true purpose that leads only to these. Your purpose may well lead to these rewards, but as a fortunate outcome, not as a goal in and of themselves alone.

The reality is that most people come at a pursuit of their purpose with the making-a-difference goal front and centre. It's often a very powerful urge, and bravo!

Others will come at their purpose with a goal still towards wealth and prosperity, and there is nothing wrong with these things at all, particularly if we are cognisant of the impacts, positive and negative, in what we do, and have a view also to be able to contribute as a consequence of our wealth.

You **are** *living a Life of Purpose*

Here's the really beautiful thing. You *are* living a life of purpose already. When it is your intention every day to live purposefully, then you've already embarked on that journey by being in the here-and-now and by simply having that intention. Intention has a powerful energy. When you desire something strongly, even if you don't know how to secure it, you are inviting the Universe to respond to you.

Living a life of purpose has a great deal to do with desire, and by our ability to go beyond ourselves for what we seek: to look to the Divine, to look at how we may serve others, to look at what contribution we can make. Everything positive we project helps to create purpose. Everything negative blocks purpose and blocks happiness.

Living a life of purpose has to do with being on the path of purpose, not having got to the end of the walk. Living our purpose has to do with allowing it to unfold, removing the obstacles to it, reinforcing its development and clarity with various daily practices, and tuning into its shifts and enhancements, throughout our lives. If your intention is to live a life of purpose, then you are.

Summary

Your purpose then is made up of these elements:
1. You have a purpose
2. Your unchanging purpose
3. Your changing purpose – developing human virtues
4. Your purpose to make a difference
5. Assisting others' purpose
6. Managing obstacles to your purpose
7. Understanding that obstacles are lessons
8. Your purpose is your passion
9. You *are* living a life of purpose already

5. Anger, Forgiveness, Depression

Purpose is a flow. And all manner of things can block that flow, but none more than these three: anger, depression, and not forgiving yourself and/or others. If depression is present, then anger and forgiveness issues will almost certainly be too. These are huge topics and I can only address them in very general terms here, and so I urge you to seek further information and support and help about this if necessary.

Depression is a major block to purpose.

The relationship of depression to purpose is a little chicken-and-egg, because an absence of purpose is one of many pathways to depression also, although rarely would it be the only one.

Of the many things that get in the way of purpose, this is arguably the biggest and hardest to see past to one's purpose. Not least of course because depression is a huge thing to get beyond just on its own.

I've had a depression. It reared its ugly head as a postnatal depression in 1998, but when I look back, knowing what I know now, I was a sitting duck with or without a pregnancy. I'd had considerable ill-health, financial stress and changes, and I'd been going a mile a minute. My body was run down and worn out.

After two years, I sought medication and it worked wonderfully. But I continued to wear myself out in all different ways, and it was many years before I really set about healing myself and those parts of me, physically, emotionally and spiritually, that continued to maintain the significant foundation for my depression to blossom. I've written several blogs about my depression; here's one: http://suefitzmaurice.com/dealing-with-depression.html

Ultimately, I got so clear on what works and what doesn't, that I put an online course together, along with my friend and colleague Sarah McCrum, to help others. It's here: http://journeytohappiness.today

> In a strange way, I had fallen in love with my depression. I loved it because it was all I had. I thought depression was the part of my character that made me worthwhile. I thought so little of myself, felt that I had such scant offerings to give to the world, that the one thing that justified my existence at all was my pain.
>
> *Elizabeth Wurtzel*
> *Prozac Nation*

For those who may be inclined to say a) there's no cure, and/or b) medication is the only cure, I'm totally with you on the value of medication – it lifts you up out of that hole for sure but it's **not** a cure. And I've seen many, many people now respond with incredible results to our healing course. (It also has a 100% money back guarantee, so what have you got to lose?)

What makes depression such a block? Because joy and happiness are significant vehicles carrying us along the path of purpose, and if you don't have them you're going nowhere fast.

Recently Sarah and I conducted a survey of people's experiences of depression and we found a whopping 44% of depression sufferers had experienced depression since childhood. That's pretty scary, isn't it? But you don't need to *keep* suffering. And if you want a future, you need to dig yourself out. Fortunately, there is a great deal of help, and increasingly more knowledge and understanding of how to do this. I hesitate to say I've found little knowledge and assistance from within mainstream medicine – I hesitate because of course it has its place – but there is no cure offered within the mainstream, and sadly also a reluctance to countenance anything alternative or that's not a chemical substance. Alternative medicines and therapies offer a great many options and I would suggest examining all of these and looking towards combinations that suit you. Our course is based on combining energy healing with diet and exercise, dealing with many of the emotional traps that have contributed to mental *and* physical ill-health, looking at the need for purpose and meaning, and daily meditation practice. We have found this to be a magical combination.

Your real self is not depressed.

It's hard to say which of the many things I've learnt about healing depression that is the most important, but if I had to single one out I'd say it's this:

Your *real* self is not depressed.

Your real self does not feel the blackness – the blackness does not exist for your real self.

To understand this, you have to have some kind of spiritual view of who and what you are, which I believe is the *real* you. I have come to recognise that there is a pure me, a Me that is in truth a spiritual being, and that the centre of that spiritual world is pure Light and that I am connected to that Light, even if I can't feel that connection most of the time. If you *know* that Light is there, then know this: your true self, the essence of who you are, is *not* depressed – it never has been and never will be. The true **You** is Light, Love, Joy and Happiness.

Joy, rather than happiness, is the goal of life, for joy is the emotion which accompanies our fulfilling our natures as human beings. It is based on the experience of one's identity as a being of worth and dignity.

Rollo May, Man's Search for Himself

If there was one thing that made a massive difference for me, it was knowing that. And then it was a short step for me to learn how to connect with the real me more and more every day and experience the reality of my naturally joyful self.

Anger

Anger comes in various shapes and sizes, large and small, aimed inwards, outwards, specifically and generally. In and of itself it's not a bad thing – there are plenty of things that happen in our lives and in the world that can make us feel angry. We can express it and let it go or we can hold onto it. Often, we hold onto it without realising. Often, we feel very justified in holding onto it, indignant at some wrong that's been committed to ourselves or others, *unwilling* to let go of what we feel is our right to our emotions and our responses.

However, there is no upside to holding onto anger. Whether aimed outwards or inwards – and self-loathing is particularly unhelpful – once it's being held rather than being let go, its energy goes from a more benign expression to something toxic and negative. And as a negative, it is simply a wall – an obstacle – to the positive flow of purpose in your direction.

The reason I've highlighted it here as a particular issue is that most people have some, a lot of people have a lot, and it can be a challenge to get rid of it. It almost always requires the assistance of a skilled counsellor or therapist to send it on its way. If it's something that's been around a while it can feel scary to let it go; it's amazing how much it defines us without us even realising it, especially if we've been hanging onto it for a very long time. The world can suddenly look very different after disconnecting from long-held anger.

If it's something that's been around you through various phases in your life, you'll probably work through many stages of releasing it – it won't all go at once. It can feel frustrating when it comes back up again, but it will probably be another layer, and the layers will get finer and less troublesome as you work through them. Once you start on that aspect of your journey, it's useful to see any recurrent arising of anger as a positive since once it comes up you can then work on letting it go. It's when it's there but it's not showing itself to you that it is truly an obstacle. All the personal work we do in this way is our gift to ourselves.

Forgiveness

Generally, hand in hand with letting anger go is the act of forgiveness, again of both ourselves and others. This is also a huge challenge and can be difficult work to do.

It's important to understand that forgiveness is not about letting someone off the hook for some ill they have done us, but rather about letting go the ties that continue to bind us to that act.

Forgiveness allows us to let go of bitterness and move on. Whether someone is punished for their act is likely not up to us, but rather it will be the job of the law, natural justice or karma. We also need to allow that process to happen in its own way, regardless of how we may want to see it unfold. When we stay attached to that outcome we stay stuck in the effects of someone's act against us and we can't move on. Forgiveness allows you to give up that process to other forces that are almost always beyond your control anyway.

Forgive yourself.

No one can live in the light all the time.

We expect perfection of ourselves too often. Partly this comes from our inability to love ourselves, at all or enough.

Remember to fall in love with yourself!

Loving yourself is a key foundation to letting go the harm others have done you, especially when you remember that *you* are holding onto *it*, not the other way around. Truthfully though, these processes of forgiveness, letting go anger, moving beyond depression, and loving ourselves, are things that happen in a concurrent swirl and spiral of moving up and out. They impact each other – let them. Anger and hurt can't occupy the same space as love very easily, so slowly make less room for them in your life by loving yourself more.

I have my doubts about the idea of forgiving but not forgetting, at least insofar as it's often expressed. If our own naiveté has led to our harm then of course we will hopefully learn and grow and won't allow that hurt to occur again. So that's an important aspect of not forgetting. But if our not forgetting has to do with remembering that specific event and the ins and outs of it and the person that harmed us, then we've probably not really forgiven. **When you get to that point where you're bored with talking about it then that's a good sign you've moved on. When you're still stuck in telling the story then you've still got work to do.**

Forgiving ourselves is important to our own well-being. As long as we're beating ourselves up – usually in our heads at 2am – we're blocking the flow of love and purpose. I always find it helpful to remind myself that there is no truth in any of the thoughts that come at 2am. If it's inspirational and feels beautiful, it might well be great, but if it's toxic and exhausting, it's crap and needs to be ignored.

Associated with self-forgiveness is often shame. It's not in the scope of this book to explore this vital topic, but if that's a part of what's going on for you then I can't recommend enough that you delve into this. Brené Brown's books are up there with the best.

Sadly, we can often double-layer all of these things – we hurt ourselves for not being able to forgive, we frustrate ourselves with our own anger and its self-sabotaging, and we feel ashamed of our shame. It's okay that you have these feelings – you remain a divine creation with or without them, beautiful to your core despite your imperfections. Start down the road of letting go what doesn't serve you and let yourself take the time you need to gently work through it all. Trust your own honest intent – the Universe will bless your self-work as long as you allow it to.

As you peel away the layers of what doesn't serve you, purpose will inherently become clearer. It can't not. When you take down the walls around your heart and soul, then that which desires communion with your heart and soul will flow in. You may feel vulnerable at first without your defences, but really, they weren't great defences because they held in the bad stuff and kept the good stuff out.

6. What purpose *is*

Primarily, purpose is to your Soul as your physical energy is to your body. It's the manifestation of who you are at your core.

Finding and Living your Purpose is a manifestation of your Spiritual Self.

Did you watch any of the Rio Olympics in 2016? It was hard to miss some of the more extraordinary talent, not to mention fabulous displays of sportsmanship: I loved the story of the New Zealand and American runners who both fell in the race and then stopped to help each other up.

When we see extraordinary physical talent, we are seeing some of the highest manifestation of our human physicality. Most of us don't aspire to quite that degree of fitness, and we can just as easily say that the ideal manifestation of our **Physical Self** is simply a fit and healthy body.

There are different ways we could define the best manifestation of our **Emotional Self**; one possibility could be to have healthy and loving relationships.

We have so many different parts to ourselves – an intellectual self, an aesthetic self – and they vary in their dominance, depending on

101

what's most important to us. An artist has a huge aesthetic self to satisfy. If they're not *doing* their art, they're less happy, less fulfilled. All of these different parts of who we are interact with each other; none is exclusive from any other part. Our physical well-being impacts our emotional well-being, and vice versa. Our general well-being is dependent on a balance of these different aspects of who we are, and not ignoring any.

We have a Spiritual Self. It's the part that looks for meaning, and its fundamental questions are *Who am I? Where did I come from?* and *Why am I here?*

I believe our Spiritual Self is the foundation of all that we are, and potentially has the greatest effect on every part of us.

Sadly, it's a part of us that's often asleep, either because we're unaware of its existence or because we deny its existence. And in denying its existence we deny access to it as the primary go-to source of meaning and purpose, denying ourselves that which is most useful to the pursuit of a better way of living.

Some people find some spiritual meaning in their religion, some ignore both religion and spirituality (generally rejecting the latter because of the former), and some may reject religion and pursue spirituality. I believe they are two very different things, although for many they will overlap.

Putting religion aside, you *have* a Soul. Since you're already aware you have a (non-physical) heart and a mind, it really shouldn't be a leap to accept this – a part of you that desires meaning in more than just an intellectual manner. It is your Soul that will reveal your purpose to you, since it already knows what it is. Whilst it's straightforward to say that we *find* our purpose, it's actually a little bit deceptive, since we know it already. Truthfully, it finds us.

To the extent that we already commune with our own Soul, we will have some connection to our purpose already; perhaps a sense of it, perhaps just the knowledge that we do indeed have one. And perhaps you already know that this is the route to revealing more of it.

> My soul is a hidden orchestra;
> I know not what instruments,
> what fiddle strings and harps,
> drums and tamboura I sound
> and clash inside myself.
> All I hear is the symphony.
>
> *Fernando Pessoa*
> *The Book of Disquiet*

Religion & Spirituality

This is a huge topic and one I could spend hours talking about; I urge you to explore this further yourself.

Religion has played a big part in my life, and I have explored many different faiths. None has given me all of the meaning I crave, although some have given me a lot of it. To the extent you may wish to understand where I, myself, am coming from, I was brought up Christian within the Anglican faith, even serving at the altar in my local Church. At 22 I became a Baha'i, a generally very humanist religion. In my mid-40s I left the Baha'i Faith in large part due to a need to explore more widely. In recent years my journey has taken me via traditional Indian (ancient Hindu) and Chinese practices and an abiding interest in Buddhism. I have learned a great deal from all of them, and each has allowed me to engage more deeply with my spirituality, although there is much that is not religious that has aided my spiritual journey also. I believe my openness to this aspect of my spiritual journey has served me in many complex ways and I could never deny the extraordinary depths and value of the religious experience in my life.

On the one hand, one might imagine that religion and spirituality ought to be the same thing. Certainly, many people experience them as such, perhaps barely discerning any distinction.

The difference is that religion is the practice of teachings set by an individual and/or institution. Spirituality is the exploration of Oneself, and the discovery and practice of one's own purpose.

To the extent that one's religion allows for and supports the inward experience, then the two overlap.

Often religion can limit our exploration of our spirituality though, perhaps because we are encouraged to *not* ask questions. Or perhaps you are encouraged to explore your own meaning in this regard. A religion that allows you to do the latter is a religion with some openness to the Truth; the former, not so much.

Understanding God is not a goal of spirituality necessarily, although it may well be an outcome.

> Spirituality is much wider than any particular religion, and even the greatest religion becomes no more than a broad sect or branch of the one universal religion, by which we understand our seeking for the eternal, the divine, the greater self, the source of unity and our attempt to arrive at some equation, some increasing approximation of eternal and divine values.
>
> *Sri Aurobindo*

Spirituality is about understanding what is meaningful to **you**; why you're here and what you're supposed to do while you're here, and what your relationship is to others, to the World and even to the

Universe. And when we come to these questions, we are coming to an exploration of our purpose.

It can also be said that **at the core of spirituality one will find love.** And in true religion I believe this is also always the core, although it's not always that aspect of religion that is made visible to outward appearances.

Let me say again: *you* may significantly find your purpose in your religion – your religion may indeed be the expression of your spirituality, and if that leaves no gap in meaning for you, then I'm happy for you. For many people this is not the case, even when religion does play a part in their life. It does no good to judge religion as lacking because of this though. Not least since the major world religions are vast, with millions if not billions of adherents and hundreds of thousands of leaders. Some religious leaders will take their flock on a journey of the spirit, whilst others will take them on a journey of dogma.

In the end, one's experience of both religion and spirituality is one's own.

I know it sounds corny, but it *is* a journey.

It's been said so many times, but it's true.

We somehow have it ingrained in us to head towards a goal with a view to that being it. That's never it. There's always more. Your purpose journey will last your whole life.

And it's also been going your whole life already, even if you didn't realise it until now. Everything, and I mean *everything*, that you've done up till now, is preparation for the rest of your journey. Use it.

Get over the idea that your life will only begin to happen when you reach your goals.
Your life is happening now,
and has been happening your whole life!

Start enjoying it! Realise that you *can* enjoy it now, even if your goals haven't arrived yet. Because for sure, **when you start enjoying it now, your goals will arrive a lot sooner**. And after those, there'll be other goals. It doesn't stop.

Ponder this:
"I believed that time was as real and solid as myself, and probably more so. I said 'one o'clock' as though I could see it, and 'Monday' as though I could find it on a map; and I let myself be hurried along from minute to minute, day to day, year to year, as though I were actually moving from one place to another. I lived in a house bricked

up with seconds and minutes, weekends and New Year's Days, and I never went outside until I died, because there was no other door. Now I know that I could've walked through the walls." ~Peter S. Beagle, *The Last Unicorn*

> **This is the real secret of life – to be completely engaged with what you are doing in the here and now. And instead of calling it work, realize it is play.**
>
> *Alan Watts*
> *The Essence of Alan Watts*

You will want to plan for your future – and so you should – but remember that the reality of life is now. If we spend our lives running away to the past and the future then we don't truly live our lives. The past is a memory; it is a thought occurring in the present, as indeed is the future. **What we have is now. And now.**

Love is the answer.

In *The Hitchhiker's Guide to the Galaxy* by Douglas Adams, the answer to everything is 42. (This is after several millennia of searching, and creating the world's biggest computer, and it leaves the custodians of the computer wondering what precisely the question was.) Correctly, the answer they should have come up with is Love.

Love is almost always the answer, and almost always the way – the method. It is the greatest power of the Universe.

We constantly block the flow of love in our own lives; because we get angry or tired or we're unforgiving or we want to make a point. We should give in to love every time.

> **We must never forget that spiritual experience is above all a practical experience of love.**
>
> *Paulo Coelho*

Love gives us the experience of joy; joy makes the Universe want to come out and play; the Universe delivers on our dreams and our purpose. It's that simple. The more I come to understand about what purpose is and how to find it, and the more people I work with, the more I come back to love.

> A life of love is one of continual growth, where the doors and windows of experience are always open to the wonder and magic that life offers. To love is to risk living fully.
>
> *Leo Buscaglia*

Love is the fuel and building block of the Universe. If not the physical universe, then that indescribable, creative aspect of it that animates all living things.

When we begin to see that every rush to judgement that blocks our ability to flow with our purpose is simply just a lack of love, that every negative thought is simply a lack of self-love, that our ability to forgive relies on our ability to experience and give love, that love really can heal, then we have to acknowledge that the root of all things probably is love.

I believe we are called upon in this century, at this time, to rise to a greater understanding of love, and particularly what the lack of it means for the world we live in now. That which is destructive and chaotic is most definitely due to a lack of love, on all our parts.

It's not an easy task. It's even harder for those mired in hate and judgement. But merely the presence of more love will ultimately make it impossible for hate to exist. This is a vital way we will all make a difference in the world: to try always to rise to acts of love; to resist the pull towards judgement, intrigue, bullying, criticism – all of which can occur at the subtlest levels in ways we are all guilty of, and that block our own purpose and therefore the opportunity to live fully. The truly rich experience is the one with *acts* of love at the foundation – not love that we simply talk about and philosophise about, but the love we *do*. Do love.

It's a feeling.

You know when you're feeling on track with your life. It feels good. It flows. Things happen. You have a sense of things unfolding for you.

You won't have reached this feeling simply because you are *doing* the right thing (ie. the right work); it will also begin to increasingly dawn on you when you have reached a certain critical mass whereby you have released a lot of your obstacles and connected more consistently with the flow of purpose in your life.

You will still have periods of uncertainty even then, but you will recognise them as moments of change and development and just go with them. You'll probably express often how great your life is!

It's unlimited.

Your purpose doesn't have any boundaries. And it has no 'end' as such. It will go on growing and changing as long as you draw breath. Purpose is not a place you get to – it's a permanent journey. And it's not simply the journey of your career – it's personal, it's spiritual, it's creative. It's your reason for becoming human.

It's the reality of who you are.

Your purpose is who you are and the more you align with it the more you'll feel yourself.

You may not feel yourself though around many of the people in your circle – friends, family, colleagues. It's difficult when you change – others either don't see the different you, or they see you but they don't know how to relate to you now. Sometimes some of the people in your life plain don't approve of what you've chosen.

This can be incredibly hurtful and saddening, especially when it's your closest friends or relatives – even your children! Our ability to let go is tested most during these times. Very often that separation will come with a great deal of criticism and baggage and projection, making it even more painful and causing us to doubt our way. It's incredibly difficult to maintain a new Self and new direction – which by their very newness are a little fragile – in the face of others' hurtful attitude or words. I think if I'd had a lot earlier the advice to a) accept that people will drop by the wayside and let go of them quickly, and b) accept that their criticisms are about them not you, then the last ten years in particular would have been a lot easier. You will not keep the same people with you on your journey throughout. Where loved ones drop away, know that new friends and guides will emerge who will travel the next part of the way with you. And they too will drop away. If you want to get what you came into this life for, trust the reality of your changing circle.

It's different every day.

You will understand clearly by now that your purpose journey keeps on changing. Truthfully, that change is pretty much a daily thing. If you're looking for a life of sameness then don't take the purpose route to it. It's not massive change on a daily basis, but there will be new opportunities, new directions, new inspiration, new ideas, daily; particularly if you follow the guidance of putting yourself in the way of inspiration, by the books you read and the people that you're around, among other things.

It's a giving-up of knowing.

You will begin to intuit your life less via your head and more via your heart and soul. And you will have less need to know precisely what's going to happen and when. When purpose comes at you on a spiritual level then you also recognise that there isn't really an end, and that it keeps on going, and that the timing of it isn't an issue. You are now living.

7. Making sure Purpose finds you

Here's the main crux of the whole thing. You need to create the conditions whereby your purpose finds you. A purposeful life is there, waiting for you, waiting for you to allow it in. These are all the ingredients required to create *the good life* – a life that has little to do with material success (albeit that you may well be more likely to achieve that in similar fashion), and everything to do with consistent happiness and fulfilment.

7.1 Some Practicalities
- Commitment.
- Start.
- Don't put things off.
- Eat better.
- Get up earlier and Get more sleep!
- You need Energy

Commitment.

I've often been a bit of an all-or-nothing person, myself. I can be either all go, or all stop. Commitment is a relative term, and we can beat ourselves up for the one area among many where we judge ourselves lacking in commitment, missing the point that we're still here and still trying to figure it out and still taking steps forward every day, slow though they may feel at times.

> Nothing in the World can take the place of persistence.
> Talent will not; nothing is more common than unsuccessful men with talent.
> Genius will not; unrewarded genius is almost a proverb.
> Education will not; the world is full of educated derelicts.
> Persistence and determination are omnipotent.
>
> *Attributed to Calvin Coolidge*

For many years, I was very ambitious and driven, but I came to see that the kind of ambition I had contained some underlying pathology of lack of confidence and a need to prove myself. I exorcised that ambition and started fresh. Overnight, I lost all ambition, and have had to find new ways to motivate myself.

Motivation comes to me now in several ways: regular meditation, surrounding myself with people who've mastered the art of commitment, the desire to create and contribute, the recognition that I have something worthwhile to say, the positive feedback of my peers and my loved ones, and by just getting on with it. Above all, the clearer my purpose is, the more inspired I am to work at it.

For a long time, I wasn't *consistent* in my work, not that that meant I was lacking in commitment especially, but over time consistency has also grown. I *write* almost every day now, regardless of what else is going on. Even if it's only a page. Generally, it's several pages.

This much I know: Keep asking questions. Keep searching. Continue where your journey takes you. Ultimately there are no failures, just the path.

**Perseverance is not a long race;
it is many short races one after another.**

Walter Elliott

Start.

I've taken on a huge new project recently, so huge it's occasionally overwhelming. It's something that's going to take a while and I just have to keep working on it each day. I remind myself daily that it's 'baby steps' that are going to get me there. Regular, consistent, and without any negative self-talk or analysis. And the thing about baby steps is, there's never been a baby that didn't stand back up again the first time they fell over. Or the tenth. Or the hundredth.

We beat ourselves up over our failure to achieve goals, but we so often seem to have expectations of achieving sometimes quite large goals in a very short space of time. *Rome wasn't built in a day.*

Set a goal and then work out what is the smallest step forward in achieving that goal that you know you can do today. And then do that. Congratulations, you're on your way to achieving your goal.

A lot of people have clarity about their purpose but find it a challenge to start walking their purpose because right now they're working another job, and they can't simply stop doing that. (We all have to do what we have to do and paying the rent and putting food on the table is generally one of them.) I wouldn't like to guess how many novels have been written on an-hour-a-day commitment, but I'd say it's a great many. I've not yet met the person who can't start moving in the direction of their purpose with a short period of committed time every day. Figure out what it is that you *can* do and start doing it.

Some of us have a lot of experience with setting goals, others less so. If you're the latter, then it's never too late to start. I have participants 70 years and older that have undertaken my purpose course. My own father told me in his 80s that he'd like to learn to meditate, and that's not the kind of thing I ever thought I'd hear from him. Start somewhere but start.

BEGIN;
TO BEGIN IS HALF THE WORK.

Don't put things off.

Unless your day's super-exciting and you're just putting off the dishes, if there's a job needs doing, do it. If it's a big job, break it down into stages and do a little each day.

Lots of people need to clean out the pile of stuff in their garages and basements and spare rooms – it always seems to be a job that gets put off and put off and put off. And meanwhile also it usually gets worse.

Start!

If you sorted a box a day, how many days are you going to need? Commit to a box a day for that many days. One box is going to take a maximum of an hour and as little as five minutes. Do it. You'll be so pleased you did.

Imagine in a month when it's all done!

What do *you* put off? Taxes, accounts, the dentist, finishing writing a book, finishing that online course you started, *starting* that online course you bought?

You can't do it all at once, but you can start. If you don't start, nothing will continue to happen.

119

Sometimes I find if my *To Do* list is too long, I don't even start it. I feel weighed down by it. So I just keep the list to a maximum of 10 things. You don't have to put everything on the list. Or create a long-term list and a short-term list, so you separate out everything that needs doing from what you can reasonably do today.

Are you putting off making up with a friend or a colleague? Are you putting off asking your boss for a raise? Are you putting off visiting a relative you don't like? Set a day, do it, don't think about it before you have to do it. When you think about it beforehand you make it bigger and scarier – we all do – the answer is to not think about it at all. Truly, it's not that hard to do.

Are you putting off quitting your job? Going back to school? Moving out? Big things like that? Well, only you can know when, but more often than not 'when' is sooner rather than later. You *may* regret taking the leap – I can't say definitively that you won't. But mostly – by a very large margin – people will say *I wish I'd done it years ago!* Follow your dreams – they're why you're here. Take the leap!

Make lists of the small things, the medium-sized things, and the big things that you've been putting off. Do one of the small things now, start on one of the medium-sized things, and do something towards one of the big things this week.

If you delay till tomorrow what ought to be done today,
you overcharge the morrow
with a burden which belongs not to it.
You load the wheels of time and prevent it
from carrying you along smoothly.

Hugh Blair
On the Importance of Order in Conduct

Eat better.

Your mind and body do not respond well to sugar, nicotine, alcohol, excessive carbohydrate, and chemical-rich 'food'. They may well be used to a diet high in these things, but I can assure you that an absence of **crap** in your diet will make you feel a whole lot better.

If you suffer from any physical ailments, chances are you will decrease your suffering with an improved diet. You will most certainly improve your mood, and if you suffer from depression you can make a dent in this too.

In addition, even limited research will give you many options for particularly healthful and cleansing elements to add to your diet, eg. foods rich in omega-3, krill for joint pain, gluten-free and ancient grains, herbal teas, and many, many other possibilities.

Your body *is* getting older and you will increasingly notice this and it will limit you more and more if you're not careful about what you put in it. Your mind does not operate independently of your body and the fuel – sluggish or rocket – that you provide it with. Nor does your soul soar on a diet of pizza, burgers, fish-n-chips and beer. You really do have to create *my body, my temple* as a foundation for a rewarding and purposeful life.

Where possible, aim to eat fresh organic food. I'm not a doctor and it's not appropriate for me to offer you medical advice, but I do recommend at least investigating natural health treatments. For example, I swear by *Golden Seal Root* now as the most powerful natural antibiotic available (not to mention good old garlic); hopefully it's not gone unnoticed by you that antibiotics are increasingly ineffective, due to overuse and increasing resistance. This is just one example of many valuable and more healthful options.

Eating better isn't just about taking the edge off your alcohol and sugar intake. Those days are gone. Nowadays we need to all but eliminate these and similar poisons from our diets, and frankly if you're over 50 you should take the view that you have little choice in the matter. When my son was 18 and 19 he lived on a diet of mostly pizza, sushi, so-called 'energy' drinks, and beer. He's extremely fit and energetic, but that won't always be the case. Don't try and have a 19-year-old's diet when you're 50!

You need Energy.

I bet you're often worn out and tired. Most of us are from time to time, and sometimes we may have felt that way for years.

That tiredness is the result of an accumulation of things: Childbirth and parenting (honestly, I reckon that's #1 for most women!), ill health, stressful relationships, hard or unsatisfying work, burning the candle at both ends, too much going on for too long, grief and loss.

All of a sudden – or maybe not so suddenly – sometime in middle age, it all just hits us and we're tired all the time. Not necessarily 'chronic fatigue' type tired, but there's a spectrum of tiredness and you know you're on it.

You need Energy. You also need to get super healthy, get some serious vitamins, do some system clean-outs (a body defrag!), stop working like a maniac and sort out your relationships. Getting some more Energy will help all those things.

Here's the simplest, quickest & cheapest way I know to do this. Get Sarah McCrum's book: *Energy on Demand.* It comes with a free online course.

We don't think much about Energy and where it comes from. It's just miraculously there, until all of a sudden, it's not. We talk about

123

there being negative and positive energy, the energy that something or someone gives off, the energy of the room, having more or less energy, something having good or bad energy.

> **Energy is the key to creativity.**
> **Energy is the key to life.**
>
> *William Shatner*

Somehow or other these are all different manifestations of the same unknown, somewhat ethereal, definitely intangible force that seems to run through every living thing, and a lot of things that aren't living at all.

What that Energy is, even science cannot fully explain. We just know that it impacts us by being less or more, good or not so good, and so on. We know when we're wasting it and we know when we need more of it. And I can tell you that at certain points, not even all the methods we have used for increasing our energy for the last few decades – sleep, certain foods, exercise – can resolve a deficit that's been accruing for all that time and is now making itself known. That's when we need to look for new ways of increasing our Energy.

Aside from strict maintenance of a super healthy routine – including sleep – you must add meditation and deep relaxation to your daily routine. Not to will be to take an inordinately longer time to bring your Energy back to a level where you can really and truly live life again.

> Energy is your 'get up and go'. It's your physical capability, your mental ability, your emotional state and your spirit. It's the essence and sum total of who you are.
>
> Energy is what gives you your capacity and motivation for life. It's the life force that flows through you and keeps you going every day. It determines your performance, your impact on the world, and your quality of life.
>
> Energy is your most precious resource.
> It responds well to being treasured,
> loved and invested in.
>
> *Sarah McCrum*
> *Energy on Demand*

Get up earlier and Get more sleep!

The healthiest and most inspirational hours of the day are the first few hours of daylight in the morning. You can tell me you're a night person till you're blue in the face – it doesn't change the fact that the best Energy of the day is in the first part of the day.

If you're already an early riser, skip ahead!

If you're awake till the wee hours, stop it!

It's *not* a good energy period of the day to be awake after midnight.

If you've got yourself into a bad habit, then work on changing it. Wake up earlier and don't nap during the day – if you stick at this long enough you'll alter your rhythm and be able to go to sleep earlier.

Simply saying you won't be able to, or insisting you're an insomniac, doesn't cut it with me, sorry. The language you tell yourself is ruling you; change it. You will be happier and healthier and more motivated in life when you can have a proper sleep cycle. Which means a proper waking up cycle too.

If you make yourself get up at 6am, you are probably going to feel like crap for a few days. That's just your body protesting. It will thank you in the long run. It's yours to command, not the other way around. Take charge!

Then make sure you're using those new early hours well. Don't use them to turn the tv on and blob out. These are some of the most useful hours you'll have in the day. Get writing, making, tidying, planning, creating, baking, cleaning, painting…

Pretty soon you're going to wish you'd done this years ago.

If you consistently skimp on sleep you are consistently putting your body under stress. If your body is under stress your mind is not at ease. And if your mind is not at ease then **nothing** else in your life will be either. And then you are in no position to be working on your purpose.

Of course, there are times in our lives when we do go without sleep for consistent periods – having a new baby is one of those. Or a sick child. Somehow Mother Nature gets us through those times, and almost certainly if you have a new baby then you're probably not thinking too much about other aspects of your purpose right now and that's probably a good thing.

If worry, deadlines, or exams, are getting in the way of your sleep, then do yourself a favour and add some meditation to some part of your day. It'll go some way to making up for the lack of sleep and it'll help ease your worry and help your mind to focus on your work.

If **getting** to sleep is your problem, there are a lot of things you can do to get better at falling asleep, not the least of which again is meditation. Almost everyone I meet who says they suffer from insomnia (most don't truly have insomnia, they just have difficulty getting to sleep) or can't get to sleep, will also tell me they've tried meditating and they can't. This is a nonsense they've told themselves. They'll usually have difficulty sleeping – and think they have difficulty meditating – because they can't switch off their brain

127

and stop thinking. That's true about the sleeping; it's not true about the meditating.

I discuss meditation further ahead, but briefly let me explain that *thinking* is a part of meditating. Thinking doesn't get in the way of meditating. But meditating sure gets in the way of not sleeping. You can learn more about meditation on my website at www.suefitzmaurice.com/how-to-meditate. You'll also find some practice meditations on the same page.

7.2 Stick with the Programme.

- Be wary of your ego.
- Go deep. (Not wide)
- Deal with your distractions.
- Focus on what you want, not what you don't have.
- Stop worrying.
- Stop sabotaging yourself.

Be wary of your ego.

I've talked about ego in Chapter 3 above but it bears repeating. It's the chief distractor from reality, truth, and our purpose. If you're being led by ambition, then you're being led by your ego. If you're being led by the idea of lots of money, then you're being led by ego. If you are ignoring reality, then you're being led by ego. If you're clinging to illusion, then you're being led by ego. Illusions can include things like belief that a non-existent relationship will solve all your problems and judging your success on the career success of others much further along on their journey than you. If there is a lot of emotion tied to outcomes, then you're being led by ego.

Ego separates you from those around you and sees progress as a contest. There is *nothing* organic or heartfelt in the way ego rules us – it over-engages our mind and our fears and rides rough-shod over our intuition. It will block your personal development, your organic growth, and your purpose.

Go deep. (Not wide.)

A factor in finding and living your purpose is your ability to do your inner work, and our inner work presents itself to us when we go deep into things. We don't meet our demons on the surface. They don't turn up in the small talk. Nor will your purpose grab you if you are only hovering around on the surface of an idea or a career possibility or a new opportunity or a possible lifestyle. Everything to do with finding your purpose involves you engaging deeply, truthfully and *soulfully*.

Don't write a book because you think you should – write it because your soul is taking you there, because you have something you *really* want to say, because you want to engage with the process of writing, not just that you want to have *written* a book (which is truthfully what a lot of people mean when they say they want to *write* a book).

There will always be aspects of your work that you *have* to do that you'd prefer not to; if you're an artist you can't just paint, you probably have to also market your work, and that probably means building a website, among other things. And these kinds of things are necessarily more superficial.

The main point here is that if you continuously flit across multiple career/job/course options, in the hope of finding the one thing that fits, then you're less likely to find it than if you go deeper into fewer areas. Anyone who has completed a university degree with a major will tell you that everything at first-year level is basic and less engaging, but at second and third year level you start to get into the nitty-gritty, the meat, the engaging level. And it continues like this into fourth year, Masters level, etc.

Relationships are also like this. We don't get challenged by our multiple casual relationships – it's the longer term, more important relationships that present us with conflicts and tensions, the need to face ourselves and the opportunity – indeed, the necessity – for personal development, growth and change.

Deal with your distractions.

Re-read Chapter 3 above and think about what might be distracting you from moving forward. Checking with yourself about what's real and what's not is a lifetime's task. And at the beginning of your journey it may even seem as though it's a full-time task. In this world of fake news and social media memes and television news soundbites, figuring out reality can be a challenge. Check in with yourself; and check in with friends who've been there and done that and live a life that proves they know which way is up.

One of the biggest distractions are other people in our lives having emotional reactions to the decisions we're making about our own lives and the way we're living them. This can be especially true if we depart from a 'normal' nine-to-five working lifestyle to pursue some other less conventional passion. One of my dearest friends lost a raft of friends and the support of most of her family when she made a massive decision to give up one career in favour of another that had been calling to her since childhood. It's the kind of reaction that can really upset our journey and it requires a tenacious commitment to ride that out. Almost always we will, eventually, find other people around us who support our new selves; it's one of the gifts the Universe delivers when we pursue our purpose.

Focus on what you want, not what you don't have.

If your Energy is focused on what you don't have and what you don't know and what the Universe isn't giving you, then you will continue to attract a don't-have, don't-know, the-Universe-isn't-giving-me existence. Ask! In fact, demand! Every day. Until you get what you want.

The Universe/God has no intention of denying you what you want, particularly as it relates to your purpose. In fact, it's as though everything you want and need in this regard is sitting there waiting for you – you just have to create the right conditions to be able to grab it. A lot of us ascribe malicious intentions to the Universe sometimes, believing it is *teaching us lessons* when we don't get what we want. The Universe doesn't perversely deny us things. Where we've got these ideas from I don't know – well, somehow, they come from our religious culture, something to do with punishment and sacrifice. I have come to understand that this is not the intention of God (or the Divine, or the Universe), but simply some other aspect of our own personal *I'm not good enough or worthy enough* story – we all have one.

Ask for what you want and know that it will come.

You won't know till you try, and all those other clichés.

Stop worrying.

In the same vein, worrying focuses our minds on what we don't want.

We've all heard of *Don't sweat the small stuff*, but honestly, don't sweat the big stuff either!

I've never been one to sweat the small stuff, but I've had my fair share of sleepless nights worrying about the big stuff, and even the big'*ish* stuff, or the stuff that was just big to me at the time, that everyone else thought I was nuts to worry about.

Have you heard the saying *Worrying is just praying for what you don't want*? Do you get what it means? It means that when you worry, you're more likely to attract the thing to you that you don't want. Truly.

Worrying is just another one of those negative influences, like anger and judgement, that get in the way of your energy flow, that get in the way of you being able to connect to your purpose and make it happen.

This is of course another one of those easier-said-than-done things, like so much else. When I realised I needed to stop doing this, one of the things I'd do is think through *What's the worst that can happen?* all the way to the end. It was rarely that bad.

Stop sabotaging yourself.

Self-sabotage is when we know we want something and then we set about making sure it doesn't happen. Or we know how to get what we want, but we do the opposite. Or simply knowing what we need to do to improve a situation and just not doing it. It's procrastinating about doing the things we know will make us happier; or waiting till circumstances are perfect before we take action. (The situation is *never* perfect.) It's when we stay in our comfort zone rather than take a risk, generally because we're afraid of failure. Or, conversely, we take needless risks and make poor decisions, attracting certain danger and negative outcomes.

Self-sabotaging behaviours cause problems and get in the way of our goals. There are obvious and especially harmful ones like drug and alcohol abuse and self-mutilation, not-quite-so harmful ones like comfort eating, over-spending and people-pleasing, and then the plain irritating (to yourself or others or both) like perfectionism, procrastinating or always saying you're sorry. This is where the expression *Shoot yourself in the foot* comes from; you won't get far with a bleeding, bullet-ridden foot.

It can help to understand **why** we do these things.

134

One reason is to avoid something unpleasant, usually feelings: sadness, anger, etc. So we drink, or we have some retail therapy or we chow down with the chocolate. My drug of choice is definitely food!

Extreme modesty and compulsive apologising are more common among women, since despite our best efforts to the contrary it's still the way society grooms us. It's going to take a while to undo the work of millennia, even when we have strong mothers and supportive fathers. It probably doesn't help the overt apologiser to tell them how annoying it is to others either – we all have that one friend that will apologise for that too. In an employment situation though they are often seen as less competent, which is when it becomes self-defeating.

Procrastination occurs in between intention and action. The problem is in not closing the space between the two. We make excuses to justify our delaying thereby sabotaging our own intention. We simply need to become aware of the need to close the gap.

I'm not convinced of the notion that self-saboteurs subconsciously have a preference for failure, but there is most definitely either a need for control, or a lack of self-worth, or both. Some have a need for excitement which can lead to undesirable outcomes. Picking fights is an example of this.

Get a handle on your own modes of self-sabotage and journal your progress with them.

7.3 Build Connection to Spirit

- Connect
- Meditate.
- Live in the present. Be here now.
- Daydream.

Connect

Give time every day to connect to the Divine. This is not simply about meditating or praying, but sitting with the Light, inviting it into your experience at that moment. If this is unfamiliar territory for you, then do understand that it is very, very simple.

You may add this into your meditation or prayer, it may be something you can do while listening quietly to some peaceful music, or you may find a quiet few minutes at different points in your day when you can do this.

Simply call on The Light. You can use a different word if your understanding of this is different – the Divine, God, Spirit… Invite that presence to be with you now. You can even *demand* it, which

136

can seem somehow unseemly or rude, but the Light is in fact ours to command. Ask for its presence and sit with it as long as you can, and allow your body, and especially your heart, to open to it. Just *be* with it.

After some practice, this can be a valuable time to ask for guidance also. Ask specific questions and really listen for the answers. If you're in doubt as to your purpose, the people in your life and things that are happening in your life, then make this time every day, to commune with the Light and to seek guidance from it.

This is one of those practices that you may or may not feel instant benefit from. If you do, fabulous; if you don't, you will within a couple of weeks. If you stick with it, it will become something you desire more and more – an addiction of sorts.

Meditate.

This is a little different from connecting, albeit that when we meditate we do indeed connect. Connection as I describe it above is something you can do anywhere in any moment. Meditation is generally something that you do for longer and in a more habitual manner; you will have a time and place where you meditate.

> Supplication, worship, prayer, are no superstition; they are acts more real than the acts of eating, drinking, sitting or walking. It is no exaggeration to say that they alone are real. ~Mahatma Gandhi

I cannot recommend enough its value. One of the keys to establishing our purpose, particularly if we're totally unclear about it, is to seek inspiration, from whatever corner it may be available. And since *finding* your purpose is mostly in fact about *revealing* your purpose, we need to connect with our own direct source of inspiration. Meditation and deep relaxation are how we do that.

To appreciate this, as I've already mentioned often (it bears repeating), we need to understand that among the different parts of who we are – physical, sexual, intellectual, emotional – we also contain a spiritual aspect, what some refer to as our Higher Self. Whatever your own personal religious and/or spiritual background, it is of value to reflect on that part of us that can enjoy a higher experience of reality. It is that part of us that is more than just some combination of our emotional and aesthetic selves that might, for example, be stirred by a beautiful sunset. It is that part of us that experiences the highest peaks of true joy, and that part of us that brings inspirational thoughts and ideas to the forefront of our minds.

Rarely do we feed this part of our Self. We understand the need to take good care of our body, that to eat more fresh fruit and vegetables and fewer processed foods is better for us, and that to exercise regularly helps us to feel energetic and maintain good health. We feed our intellectual needs with books and learning. We develop our emotional Self in positive relationships and overcoming emotional limitations and fears. Our spiritual Self is fed principally by firstly creating a foundation of health and wellbeing in those other aspects of our Self, and then largely by meditation and deep relaxation.

> The old dispute about the relative virtues of the active way and the contemplative way is a spurious one. We require both. They are phases of a single rhythm like the pulsing of the heart, the in-drawing and letting go of breath, the ebb and flow of the tides. So we go deep, deep inwards in meditation to consolidate our vital energy, and then, with greater love and wisdom, we come out into the family, the community, the world.
>
> *Eknath Easwaran*
> *God Makes the Rivers Flow*

There are many varied ways to meditate. I offer a free set of guided meditations on my website, along with some basic instruction about meditation.

Meditation is generally understood as a practice to train the mind, and this produces a little bit of misunderstanding of the broader value of meditation, and especially of *how* to meditate. The difficulty with thinking of meditation as a mind training technique is that people then consider themselves to have failed the moment they start to think, and this is unfortunate since thinking is realistically a part of meditation. So the first thing I always say to people is that you should expect to think, potentially the entire time you're meditating, and that's not a bad thing.

> Perhaps the most important thing one can discover through the practice of meditation is that the self – the conventional sense of being a subject, a thinker, an 'experiencer' living inside one's own head – is an illusion.
> ~Sam Harris

There are many forms of meditation but the simplest and most common is a light focus on a word (a mantra), or one's breath, or possibly a picture in one's mind's eye of, say, a candle.

What you can expect to gain from meditation over time will generally include a greater sense of physical and emotional well-being, greater calm (less panic & anxiety), and an improved connection to the expression of love, compassion and other similar virtues. Different types of meditation may develop these or other outcomes more or less.

In my life I have practised three very specific, very different forms of meditation:

One has been prayer, and even within that I have found great variety in my own and others' understandings, techniques and practices. I now prefer to hear prayer rather than say it myself; I like the quiet spaces between the words and I find a lot of peace there.

In my twenties, I learnt *Transcendental Meditation*, a specific technique with a mantra, based on the teachings of Maharishi Mahesh Yogi, taught throughout the western world to millions and millions of people over several decades – made especially famous by The Beatles' visit to Maharishi in the late 1960s.

In my forties, I learnt a method of deep relaxation that is based on a knowledge of the energy and light that underlie all things, and it comes from the Chinese tradition of *qigong*.

I've also learned breath techniques.

In terms of their outcomes, none have been especially different than any other form. It's fair to say I've also found via them a method by which I may make a difference in lives other than my own, and the understanding of how this is so. This is quite reasonably understood as the result of a developing compassion and the knowledge of the unity of all things.

It is a goal of most religious prayer and meditative practice to affect the world and people beyond just oneself. To the extent that we, as individuals, are able to engage in meditative techniques, we are able to not only influence our own health, well-being, good fortune, happiness, and purpose; but also that of others around us, and indeed the whole world. And who of us does not have a responsibility to contribute to that spirit in every way we can?

> Mindfulness is not at all a mystical state beyond the reach of the average person. It is something quite simple and common and very familiar to us. ~Nyanaponika, *The Heart of Buddhist Meditation*

Avoid judging your meditation as good or bad or something else. There is no bad meditation. Meditation just is, and it will work its magic whether or not you enjoyed it more or less. Sometimes you can *feel* so connected, you can even waft away into nothingness for a time, and half an hour can go by without you realising. These seem like great meditations, but whilst they are enjoyable they are not greater or lesser than any other. The murky-feeling, disturbed meditation can still have a very powerful effect on you – that may be why it feels less glowing – there can be a lot of *gunk* being removed; you just don't know, so don't entertain these thoughts of good or bad. They have no value and just diminish the experience.

Live in the present.

This is one of those oft-repeated phrases like *love yourself* and *let it go* which most people ought to respond to with a) What does that *mean*?! and/or b) Yes, but *how*?! because it's just not enough on its own to tell people these things without explaining how and why.

142

Notwithstanding the need to learn from the past and set goals for the future, living in the present means being able to fully experience and take joy in what's happening right now; being aware of what's around us, being present with other people, being conscious of our own thoughts and emotions and responding to them with a mind and heart that are unattached to things not in the here and now.

When we live in the here and now, free from expectations, free from the stories we tell ourselves about ourselves, we can simply enjoy now. And in that way we also create a better future. The future is built entirely on now, and now, and now… When you are your best self now, you will become the best you in the future.

The reality is that none of us is our best self in every moment, so there's no point beating yourself up about that. But we can work on it when we remember to. And over time there are a number of things we can do to help us live now.

Daydream.

Remember how you used to do so much of this when you were a teenager? About the life you were going to have, and who you were going to marry, and the holiday you were going to go on? All those things?

Do that again.

Give yourself 5 or 10 minutes in the day, every day, to just sit, close your eyes and dream. *Make* yourself do it. Don't let the pressure of whatever else you have to do today get in your way. Try to sit calmly without that pressure making itself felt in your daydreaming.

Make sure there's no one around and you won't be interrupted. If you journal, then write down the daydreams you have during these times. (If you don't journal, you might like to start; you'll have other things you'll want to write down before you've got to the end of this list.)

It's really important you don't analyse your daydreams or give them ratings about how much you like them and especially not how likely you think they are to happen or not happen. All of that left-brain stuff has to keep out of this. This is *only* about daydreaming.

The value of this regular exercise is in allowing yourself to have big, bold ideas; and the more you do this, the more big, bold ideas you'll have and the more comfortable you'll get to be with having them.

As we get older, we forget to daydream. Or we consign daydreaming to our youth, thinking we've grown up now. In this respect, we should never grow up. **Forgetting to daydream lowers our expectations of what's available to us in our life**, and then that in turn reduces what *becomes* available to us. You will open the door to more by entertaining the pictures of it in your mind.

144

7.4 Do It Differently

- The Universe wants to play.
- Courage is the foundation of all change.
- Creativity.
- Experimenting.
- Create a joy-filled experience.
- Change the way you do things.
- Do something that scares you.
- Go on an adventure.
- Don't worry about uncertainty.
- Having a Big Vision and not playing small

The Universe wants to play.

I've come to believe that *God/the Universe/the Divine/...* wants most of all to 'play' with us. It wants to engage, to have fun, to do a dance with us, to skip down the path of our life whistling a happy tune.

And, the more we take an attitude of play and the more we focus on enjoyment, the more the Universe comes out to play.

And the bigger our goals are, the more the Universe stumps up and supports us in those goals.

My spiritual experiences over many decades have left me with no doubt that the Universe has a sense of humour and a sense of fun, and that its primary energy of Love is a spirit-filled, dancing, loving Energy, that likes nothing more than our happiness; in particular, the happiness that comes from finding and living our purpose.

So, the more we focus on joy, the more we set *silly* (ie. huge) goals – the more we take an attitude of *play* towards our life and our purpose – the more the Universe steps up to help us make that happen.

Joy and Love are very closely related. One invites the other.

So, make **joy** a key goal of every day, and understand that the sillier your goals, the more likely the Universe is to support you in them.

> Hindus, when they speak of the creation of the universe call it the play of God, the 'Vishnu lila', *lila* meaning play. And they look upon the whole universe as a play, as a sport, as a kind of dance. *~Alan Watts*

I've had clients over the years with some really massive goals. One of my clients wants to totally alter the landscape of a particular social issue in her entire country. As soon as she became clear on that goal – huge though it was – *the very next day* synchronicities began to occur that demonstrated the Universe was already stepping up to play.

When you have a goal that is realistically beyond the ability of a single person to achieve, then you *need* the Universe to help you. And that's the value of a big goal, because you can only achieve it with divine assistance, and there's nothing the Divine likes more than to assist – or more to the point, play.

PLAY!
INVENT THE WORLD!
INVENT REALITY!

Vladimir Nabokov
Look at the Harlequins!

Courage is the foundation of all change.

This is one of my favourite quotes. I have it on my email signature, and it's one of my own signature strengths and one of the characteristics most people tend to use in describing me.

We have to be brave to try something new. There is nothing will lead you to your purpose faster than doing something different.

It takes courage to endure the sharp pains of self-discovery rather than choose to take the dull pain of unconsciousness that would last the rest of our lives.

Marianne Williamson

People are forever leaving the comment *Easier said than done* in my Facebook page comments on posts that exhort people to do something that's different for them. Please get this straight:

***Everything* is easier said than done.**

It is the single most pointless excuse I've ever seen or heard. And nobody ever said any of it was easy anyway. Although, I'll tell you this for free:

Most things aren't as hard as you think.

How often have you said to yourself or others *wow, that wasn't as hard as I thought it would be?* How often have you got to the other side of something challenging and wondered why you didn't try it years ago?

If you want your life to be different, you have to change some things. Change is accompanied by discomfort. (Often that's putting it mildly!) To face that discomfort requires courage.

> Life entails courage,
> or it ceases to be life.
>
> *E.M. Forster*
> *Pharos and Pharillon*

I have always, without exception, found reward in finding courage. Particularly when it comes to facing up to myself. I'm not a bad person, but *ewww* I've found some things about myself that disgust me. When you first realise them, you just do **not** want to go there. But they never look that nasty from the other side.

So my best advice is to always face up to your own shit.

The other courage we need is to take risks, face down challenges, get out there and go for it. You will rarely regret taking the leap.

> Without **courage,**
> we cannot practice any other virtue with consistency.
> We can't be kind, merciful, generous, or honest.
>
> *Maya Angelou*

Creativity.

There are many answers to the question *Why are we here?*
We can say we are here to find and live our purpose; we can say we are here to love whoever is around to be loved; we can say we are here to enjoy ourselves; we can say we are here to make a difference to the world. They're all great answers.

If you understand the power of the Universe to go on creating itself, then it surely follows that we are here to do the same, whether to follow some universal example of creation or whether it's simply a part of our nature. Either way, it seems fundamental to our existence. We are here to create.

> Living creatively
> is really important to maintain
> throughout your life.
> And living creatively doesn't mean
> only artistic creativity,
> although that's part of it.
> It means being yourself,
> not just complying with the wishes
> of other people.
>
> *Matt Groening*

At times when I've felt under some pressure to live up to an obligation to contribute to the world, it made so much difference to re-organise that idea into the notion of being creative. To simply create something. For surely it would make a contribution anyway, or at least lead to a contribution. And it felt more fun and less like a duty. I'm not always so good with duty. If there's some societal expectation to do something or other, then I'm very likely to want to do the very opposite.

Creating isn't simply about producing art or building a house or creating some *thing*; when you provide a service to someone you're creating something. Doing the dishes is creating – it's creating order. Providing a listening ear is creating – it's creating love and kindness and understanding. We're creating all the time without realising it.

All creation moves in the direction of purpose. When we can see the reality and power and truth of creating, then we can set about being more deliberate about it and moving ourselves more in the direction of our own purpose via the vehicle of creation.

> Creativity itself doesn't care about results – the only thing it craves is the process. Learn to love the process and let whatever happens next happen, without fussing too much about it. Work like a monk, or a mule, or some other representative metaphor for diligence. Love the work. Destiny will do what it wants with you, regardless.
>
> –Elizabeth Gilbert

Experimenting.

THINGS DON'T JUST HAPPEN, THEY ARE MADE TO HAPPEN.

John F. Kennedy

If you've got to this point in reading, then this shouldn't come as a surprise. The thing is, if you're not clear on your direction, it generally doesn't matter *what* you do, as long as you do something. The simple act of doing will produce some energy for your purpose journey.

Here's the really interesting thing, and this will be true for a lot of people...

I'm 55. When I was at primary school (elementary school), I wanted to be a doctor. I don't know quite what happened when I got to high school but I was extremely disinterested and never had anything like the grades I needed to get into medical school. After I left high school, my mother made me do a secretarial course. Quite an extreme change. Actually, I really liked it and I went on to have various office jobs over the next few years, culminating in working for a law firm in Sydney, from which I decided to launch myself into law school. Then my mother died, and lo and behold I decided to become a nurse. (My mother was a nurse – kind of Freudian, right?) From there I went into the medical industry selling medical equipment, ultimately having my own multi-million-dollar company. Then I had children, became a part-time farmer, went back to university, became a CEO for a large not-for-profit, became a business consultant, became a CEO again for a training company, wrote a novel, got into social media, started coaching, wrote another book, and it'll change again yet.

My point is, nobody could have predicted any of that, least of all me. But I can look back on all of it and see so much value. Not least of all that I can type really fast.

Just do it. Doesn't matter what *it* is.

> A man who waits to believe in action
> before acting is anything you like,
> but he's not a man of action.
> It is as if a tennis player
> before returning a ball
> stopped to think about his views
> of the physical and mental advantages of tennis.
> You must act as you breathe.
>
> *Georges Clemenceau*

Create a joy-filled experience.

At the centre of all that is perfect in the Universe are joy and love. When your heart is expanded and filled with these, then you are closer to that which expands and fills your life generally.

Genuine joy and love create the river upon which every other good thing is carried into our life. So the more we create opportunities to experience joy, the more good we experience in our life. And that same river will carry the detritus of our life away with it too.

Write a list of what makes you happiest and try to create as many of these experiences each week that you can. Here are a bunch of possibilities to get you started:

- Beautiful movies: *Chocolat, Avatar, Boy, Whale Rider*...
- Funny movies: whatever makes you laugh out loud – the best laugh I had in the last few years was *Heat*. I've watched it four or five times and I still laugh out loud!
- Walking in nature, on your own or with a special friend.
- An art exhibition.
- A play or a concert.
- An evening with friends you love, who love you.
- A couple of hours in the garden.
- Painting or photography, or some other art you enjoy. (Adult colouring books are a wonderful new invention!)
- Cuddling your grandchildren and reading them a story.
- Cuddling your dog and listening to Mozart or Puccini.
- Meditation.

Change the way you do things.

Do you always have the same morning routine? Always drive to work the same way?

It may sound kind of inane but do it differently.

You'll be amazed what a small shift like that will do. You'll enjoy it. It'll take you out of yourself in some small way.

Work up to changing the way you do some bigger things.

Journal a plan to do something a different way every day. Watch what fresh energy this brings into your day.

Do something that scares you.

Okay, so I don't want you to get frightened out of your skin and have a heart attack! I'm not talking *that* scary.

What are the things you put off doing because they have an element of fear or uncertainty to them – the ones that if you 'fail' you'll feel like an idiot or at least not very bright or you think you'll stutter or won't know what to say, or something unknown that you don't want to explore because whatever it is it's terrible.

So there's the things you pretty much *have* to do, because they're really essential for you to get on with what you want. And then there's the things you *would* do if you had a little more courage.

Let me tell you that VICTORY IS YOURS and it's just on the other side of what you're afraid of.

I'm not talking procrastination here – I'm talking fear – although the two overlap a lot of the time.

And whilst I said I'm not suggesting you frighten yourself out of your skin, there is something to be said for the odd daredevil experience like bungee jumping or sky diving to really let you know you're alive!

Generally, the kind of things I'm talking about though, include:

- Calling someone to ask for help of some kind.
- Just asking for help!
- Putting yourself forward, perhaps on social media – for example, a number of people have changed the name of their business Facebook pages to include their own name and photo.
- Seeking to publish your book, your poetry, your art – letting the world see it.
- Quitting your job or asking for reduced hours to be able to pursue something you love.
- Insisting on your *you* time – something many mothers especially are often slow to do.
- Committing to take that course that's going to help you develop the thing you love – your commitment might be about the time, the money, or just the act of going back to school.

Go on an adventure.

Size doesn't matter!

I've been on several really big adventures, and a lot of small ones. Anything that takes you somewhere new, outside your usual routine, and generally involves potential for the unexpected.

My best – ie. most memorable – adventures have been rafting the Grand Canyon, traveling the globe with my teenage daughter, my first visits to Ireland and Scotland, and what we came to refer to as *The Accidental Mary Pilgrimage*,[3] a trip through France and Spain with a friend. But the small adventures are legion and require few dollars, if any, and just a bit of imagination. The right choice of company is imperative.

Money *can* be an object to grand adventures, but it's amazing what you can do with little or nothing, except your time and energy.

Big adventures will usually take us somewhere so different as to have a profound impact on how we view the world and can take us so far out of ourselves that we view our own smaller world differently – these are ideal opportunities to look at our life, our goals, where we're at, and where we'd like to be. It's harder to have this perspective when we're in the thick of our own life.

---

[3] Published on Amazon at https://amzn.to/2L87XDF

When we're on adventures we're usually reminded of how much we like them and how we ought to plan them more often, and how we need to alter our life around to make that happen. Almost everyone I know wants more time for fun, and too many people *dream* of making that happen without actually *making* it happen. Remind yourself of the need to make it happen by taking more adventures. Pretty much no one ever regretted a great adventure.

Don't worry about uncertainty.

Or what to do when it all turns murky.

Purpose doesn't go in a straight line. Nor is it consistently present. It's not the easiest of trails to follow and you can frequently feel as though you are off the path, lost, with no sense of which way to go to get back on the path again. Life is like that, and so is your purpose.

Think back on a tough time you've had in your life but you got through to the other side of it. When you were in that tough time you probably had no idea of the way out and through, but you got through anyway. You probably didn't even get through in a way you could have predicted, otherwise you might have found that route and got out sooner.

Every situation that comes along is new. We don't ever stop learning. We do however get wiser and smarter and more intuitive and we can often get through a lot more things a lot more quickly, with experience.

I've realised, when I'm feeling in the middle of a fog with no sense of direction (it happens more often than you might think), there are several useful and simultaneous responses:

1. Be patient. I've realised the Universe is on my side, and it's often been the case that when I'm unclear the Universe is in fact busy creating something new for me.
2. Think about what the situation is teaching you. Maybe there's something, maybe not, but it's always good to look.
3. Do *something*. All activity towards your purpose is good activity, even if you're not sure of the direction. It will become clear, and in the meantime the Universe will step up to play with us if we're taking action. If we drop out and do nothing, it will tend to do nothing too.
4. Meditate. Or some activity that connects you to Source. If we're in a fog, meditation can feel hard work and not feel like it's bringing us any inspiration. It *will* be working though – that's what meditation does. Keep it up and give it time.

In one way, you're never really off the path. Your whole life is your purpose. But if you've been active in pursuing your purpose then you certainly need not worry that clarity will be yours again soon.

Having a Big Vision and not playing small.

There is magic in having a vision for something that has some impossibility about it. Marianne Williamson says it best:

> Our deepest fear is not that we are inadequate.
> **Our deepest fear is that we are powerful beyond measure.**
> It is our light, not our darkness that most frightens us.
> We ask ourselves, 'Who am I to be brilliant,
> gorgeous, talented, and fabulous?
> Actually, who are you not to be? You are a child of God.
> Your playing small does not serve the world.
> There is nothing enlightened about shrinking so that other people
> will not feel insecure around you.
> We are all meant to shine, as children do.
> We were born to make manifest the glory of God that is within us.
> It is not just in some of us; it is in everyone and as we let our own
> light shine, we unconsciously give others permission to do the same.
> As we are liberated from our own fear,
> our presence automatically liberates others.
>
> *Marianne Williamson*

What Marianne's words don't go on to convey is the pure magic that arises from deciding to play big, and here I'm referring to the desire of God/the Universe/Life to engage with the playfulness and joy of goals that can only really be achieved with that engagement.

'We were born to make manifest the glory of God that is within us' could also be said: *We were born to achieve the impossible.* That is the power with which we are endowed as human beings.

Almost all of us constrain and reduce the size of our own potential world, life and experience.

Generally, it's difficult to conceive of a bigger life if we've not lived a bigger life; and we tend to think our lives smaller as we get older. It's easier to have big dreams when we're younger, but somehow at some point those dreams vanish.

When we do try and think bigger, aside from how difficult it can be, it's very difficult to follow through and maintain a bigger vision.

The reality is we have to learn to do things in stages. None of us stood up for the first time as babies and then straight away ran to the other side of the room. When we first stood up we probably didn't even conceive of running to the other side of the room. The very idea of running probably didn't exist in our consciousness. And yet now, well we may not be able to run very far at this point in our lives, but most of us can run. We may not even think twice about it.

Thinking a bigger life likewise takes stages in our vision; stages we either lost when we were younger, or stages we never got to because we just stopped going bigger at some point.

So you have to practice expanding your vision.

What's the next biggest stage your life could take? In terms of income, lifestyles, career, purpose, relationship…? How about increasing your income by ten per cent? And then when you get used to the idea that that's *possible*, whether or not you increase your income by five, ten or twenty per cent, then expand your idea of what's possible to another stage again.

Picture this new and bigger view of your life whenever you can remember to. Write about it in your journal every day.

7.5 Let It Flow

- Don't expect to know everything.
- Stay curious.
- Be comfortable with contradiction.
- Change the way you look at things.
- Don't resist change.
- Trust the Universe.
- Ask for your purpose.

Don't expect to know everything.

All the details of your purpose journey are never going to be available to you all the time. In fact, *all* the details won't be available *any* of the time. This would be like knowing your whole life's journey now and we all know that's not going to happen. Amazingly though, you'll probably expect to have more information about your purpose at certain points than you'll actually have. Hopefully you will have what you need in that particular moment, and the rest will unfold as you go along. Don't let the lack of information stop you. Remember the Universe will assist you more the more you take action yourself. There will *always* be unknowns, in everything you do; it's an unrealistic and poor excuse to use the unknown as an obstacle to continuing.

Having said that, you'll have occasional periods of huge fog. I've come to see this as a very normal part of your purpose journey, and rather than being an obstacle I've learnt to see these periods as in fact very important. I'll talk more about periods of considerable fog further ahead, but in brief, let go an anxiety around this as that only serves to block the flow of purpose further.

163

Stay curious.

Curiosity is a natural trait of higher functioning animals and especially humans. It's how we learn. It's uniquely powerful in the young and tends to decrease and stagnate over time. It serves to stimulate many aspects of our Self, intellectually, artistically, emotionally, spiritually, physically, etc. We can *make* ourselves learn new things, but without our natural curiosity it's a whole lot harder – it feels like a grind. Without curiosity, life is dull; and that dullness is visible in much of the human race every day and it rapidly turns to desperation, depression and disease. And from depression and dullness it is very difficult to resurrect curiosity.

Stay curious! If it requires effort, then make that effort, even if in only the smallest ways. Examine the news, not for what's repeated every day, but for the new and exciting things – the ideas, the people doing things differently, the new discoveries. Read fiction and non-fiction from genres you wouldn't normally choose. Take on new activities and interests; talk to new people and ask them about themselves and their lives. Your curiosity will stimulate you; it will bring new and useful ideas and people your way, and with the Universe on your side some of the things that come your way will almost certainly support you in your purpose. Curiosity has rewards!

Be comfortable with contradiction.

Actively work to remove yourself from the pressure to polarise yourself. That pressure is seen most clearly in the political realm and in that arena it's massive. The politically polar positions of left and right today present one of the greatest falsehoods in our lives and one of the most difficult to resist. This is not to say that we shouldn't reject things like bullying and fascism – of course we should – but the designation of 'left' and 'right' isn't useful in reality and presents a false demarcation of values that tends to bind us to a 'side', and sides can tend to be more destructive than constructive.

More commonly we'll be presented with what on the face of it may seem like opposing options. But the truth is these can often more easily coexist than we think. Often there's a seeming contest between what could be thought of as spiritual principles versus practical principles, like the many examples I give in chapter 3. It's okay for these apparent opposites to sit there – we don't have to resolve the contradiction, despite the compulsion to do so. Learning to sit comfortably with contradiction – allowing two or more opposing ideas to exist in our mind at the same time – is not only a sign of a mature mind but it will also lead us to new and more worthwhile truths, not least because we're not putting up a fight against them. Being open-minded includes being open with our own thinking, not just other people's.

Change the way you look at things.

It's so important to be able to go *What if...?* and look at things from another perspective. You don't have to hold to a particular belief yourself to still be able to consider what that belief is all about and what the world looks like from that perspective. **Most humans are wedded to their own particular perspective on just about everything, and as a result we all limit our own possibilities for change, and thus also for growth.**

Our beliefs are unique to each of us, more unique than our DNA. There are no two people that hold the identical set of beliefs. Therefore it can be reasonably concluded that no one holds a 'correct' set of beliefs. Do you see how important that simple fact is to being able to accept the value of looking at things differently?

I'm often irritated by comments from people responding to a particular poster I've put on one of my Facebook pages – say for instance a quote from Einstein or Wordsworth or Gandhi... And someone will write *Wrong!* And maybe they'll give a reason and maybe they won't. And I think to myself, good grief! It's Gandhi! Who are you to write *Wrong!* to something Gandhi said?! Of course everyone is entitled to their opinion, that's not my point – my point is: try it on for size, think about it, consider why Gandhi would have said that, *know* that Gandhi was someone who thought a lot about these kinds of things over many years, that he had a well-trained mind and a very developed spiritual life.

There is so much division in the world right now – between religious views, political views, between races, and still even between the genders. People are fixed to their views and fear unknown forces if they change them. It is a rare few that are capable of looking at others' perspectives honestly, without fear, and with grace. To learn to do so is incredibly freeing, not least from one's own beliefs. We should *always* be prepared to change our beliefs. Contrary to the opinion of many, it is *not* going to bring down bolts of lightning upon you if you *look at* alternative beliefs, with a view to *understanding* them. It is a sign of intelligence to be able to hold two or more contrary perspectives in one's thoughts at the same time – doing so doesn't mean you have to let go of your own beliefs – it does mean you appreciate that there is a lot more wisdom in the world than just that which you hold to yourself.

Don't resist change.

Don't get in the way of your own purpose
by resisting change.

Since change will occur anyway, it's not useful to try to resist it – you will simply find yourself well and truly behind, and in the process you will block the flow of purpose towards you. Your purpose will necessarily bring change in your life – if you're not living your purpose now, and you want to be, then some things will have to change – that's simply logical. So don't get in the way of that.

> The universe is change;
> our life is what our thoughts make it.
>
> Marcus Aurelius
> *Meditations*

Trust the Universe.

Feel free to use a different word instead of *universe* – God, Goddess, the Divine, Source, the Creator, Mother Nature, Energy, the Energy Field, or something else that may suit you better. We all have different explanations for this and words are important; (although it's also good not to let them become an obstacle). If you don't have a belief in any such power, well, try it on for size, just for now.

Most people believe in some Creative Force that they also believe is much, much, much greater than them. Myself, I believe I'm a part of that Creative Force which for now I'll call the Universe. I also believe that the Universe helps steer me in the direction of my purpose. And so, with that in mind, one of the things I need to learn to do is let go some of my own plans and designs sometimes and let the Universe lead me there instead. Not least because, when we insist on taking everything into our own hands, we can actually block the Universe's power to support us.

Pretty much every spiritual view of the world that anyone I've ever met has, involves a belief in the power of some Greater Force. It would be a bit contradictory therefore to not also *trust* in that Force, or to not accept that it has something good in store for us. Now this doesn't mean that we should *only* trust in the Universe; the Universe requires us also to take action – that's key to engaging with the Universe and working *with* it. Sometimes though, you really have to get out of your own way.

Particularly when we're in a state of change, or on the cusp of change, it's often the case that we have multiple major decisions facing us simultaneously and it can be extremely stressful. *Shall I leave my job? Shall I go back to school? Shall I leave my marriage? Should I move towns?* That kind of thing. We easily wind ourselves up in knots trying to figure out the right thing to do. Stop. Just stop. If you've thought every possible thing you can about it then stop trying to make a decision. Let it all be and give it over to the Universe. Give the Universe time. And then wait patiently. Or as patiently as you can. It's been my experience that it will always become obvious.

> Patience, n. A minor form of despair, disguised as a virtue.
>
> Ambrose Bierce,
> *The Devil's Dictionary*

Ask for your purpose

If you're not clear what your purpose is, or you want your purpose to happen, *ask* the Universe for help. Ask for clarity, ask for the things you want to unfold to do so. You don't have to know how that's going to happen for it to indeed happen.

If you feel like you've been trying to figure out your purpose for a long time then spend every day – every moment that you remember – asking the Universe for clarity. If you also meditate regularly and do other things that allow you the opportunity to build that connection with the Divine, then not only will the Universe respond but you'll hear it. You'll receive the ideas and inspiration you've been waiting for because you've opened yet another door to being able to hear what the Universe has in all likelihood been busy telling you all the time but you've not been listening.

Most of us don't ask for help when we need it. When it comes to something as intangible as our purpose, we never think to ask. And yet it's always so obvious that we should. We don't know everything on our own; we often look to the Divine for inspiration and guidance and then wonder why we're not being 'told', when we haven't actually asked the question. It's like that old joke of continuously asking God to let you win the lottery and God eventually tells you "For Heaven's sake, buy a ticket!"

7.6 LET YOURSELF OFF THE HOOK

- You have to love yourself first.
- Speak sweetly to yourself.
- Be grateful.
- Believe in yourself.
- Stop worrying.

You have to love yourself first.

You really do!

> Self-love is the source of all our other loves.
>
> *Pierre Corneille*

The thing about this though, is that although we hear it all the time, no one ever tells us ***how*** to love ourselves. Here are some starting points.

1. It works well if you understand that you're a spiritual being living a physical life, and that necessarily that spiritual being is perfect in every way. Isn't that a great place to start?!

2. Forgiving yourself for everything you've done 'wrong', or that you *think* you've done 'wrong'.

3. Nothing's really wrong. We make mistakes to learn. Our actions are those of our physical being, not our spiritual being which is perfect. Our spiritual being, and all other spiritual beings, have already forgiven us for everything we've done or will do. That is their nature.

4. Spoiling yourself with treats (especially if those treats are binges of food and alcohol) is not how you love yourself. It's not called 'spoil' for nothing.

5. Treating yourself with *truly* joyful experiences (ie. not binges of food and alcohol) is one way to love yourself. Since this is what you should do every day, it's not really a treat.

6. Make a regular daily practice of affirming how much you love different parts of you, your body & your character.

That's a start…

Loving yourself is a way of engaging with the Divine, which is essentially Love also, and thus creating a connection that helps to put you in the flow of your purpose.

> We can climb mountains with self-love.
> ~*Samira Wiley*

Speak sweetly to yourself.

Imagine you are the person you love more than anyone else in the world. Most of us don't view ourselves that way. We tend not to like ourselves very much and we generally hold ourselves to impossible standards all the time, standards that we can only fail to meet, at least in our own heads. (Paradoxically we tend to defend ourselves more vigorously in relation to others.)

We almost always wish we were prettier, smarter, nicer, more likeable – generally just more of everything. None of us would ever talk down to the people we love like that, so it's extraordinary that we do it to ourselves. Despite what we think, this is not actually how we're going to make ourselves better at anything. The reverse in fact is true: you will become more when you appreciate yourself, compliment yourself, love yourself, express gratitude for all that is wonderful about yourself, and indeed for all that isn't so wonderful even (or that you perceive as being not so wonderful.)

This isn't at all easy to do. Among the many things I recommend people do to start delivering their own life of purpose, changing the way we think *is* one of the harder ones. The constant hammering we give ourselves is just that, constant.

Every time we speak against ourselves in our own heads we're picking a fight with our own chances of success.

173

Whenever you remember to, make a point of appreciating something about yourself, preferably several things, since you may not remember to do it that often. If you journal and/or meditate regularly, these are ideal moments to add in a little self-love and self-appreciation time to your day.

You will find there are layers and layers to your dislike and criticism of yourself. It's almost as though you figure out the bigger picture stuff but then there's a layer of finer detail pops up soon after, often more quietly. Truly, it's very sneaky this stuff. It's fought hard to have a place in your mind and it won't go easily. But it will eventually give way when you fill your mind with love and sweetness for yourself.

Be grateful.

For me this used to be like those *Love Yourself!* memes on social media. Everyone's always going on about how important it is to be grateful, to express your gratitude, *blah blah blah*. And I was always like *Meh!* Not my thing.

> Acknowledging the good
> that you already have in your life
> is the foundation for all abundance.
>
> Eckhart Tolle

Then enough people I really respected were on about it so much that I thought I'd give it a go. And I can tell you, it really works. The thing that works about it is that a) it makes you happier, and b) you begin to experience your life as one that is filled with abundance, and the more you do that, the more abundance you also attract to you. It's incredibly simple and incredibly powerful. It's an important key in opening yourself up to the flow of your own purpose.

There are a few ways to do this and you should probably give all of them a bit of attention.

1. Most straightforward is to express your gratitude for the **good things you have**. You can do this:
   a. When you remember, or
   b. You can keep a daily journal where you express these things

2. Write down all the **things you don't like** about
   a. Your life
   b. Your body

And then express your gratitude for those. Why? Let me give you some examples. 1. I don't have long, thin, glamorous legs – I really wish I did. But I am soooo grateful I have legs, and I'm so grateful I have *strong* legs that are healthy. 2. I don't own a big house. Actually, I'm kinda happy right now that I don't own a big house – I used to own a big house and it was like an albatross round my neck. I was soooo grateful for the cute cottage I lived in – it was in the countryside and there were sheep and lambs and native birds all around. It was so peaceful; and being small it was really easy to have it clean and tidy. It was light and airy – in fact I could go on and on about my beautiful little cottage. Not to mention that I'm just soooo grateful that I had a roof over my head at all! Let alone that it was such a lovely one. Now I travel and I live in other people's houses and in hotels and *B&Bs* and I have so much freedom and joy from it all that I can't imagine being anywhere for too long these days, but one day I'll have that cottage again. Get the picture?

3. In any and every moment that you feel low, express your gratitude for something good in your life; you will find with not much practice that you'll shift to a higher place.

A grateful heart cannot, in the moment of its gratitude, be unhappy or sad. So it is a unique tool in so many ways. Add it to your daily life as often as you can remember.

> Nine-tenths of wisdom is appreciation.
> Go find somebody's hand and squeeze it,
> while there's time.
>
> *Dale Dauten*

Believe in yourself.

You are as capable as anyone else of success, and the obstacles in your way are as small or as great as anyone else's. If your sense of your own value and success is based on what others say to you and about you, then your self-worth and success will forever be precarious. You *must* believe in *yourself.* When you learn to strengthen your own sense of your self – your own power – then there's no limit to not only what you can achieve, but what you will *know* you can achieve.

Your true inner Self – or your Higher Self – has ultimate faith in you; you are only hampered in your self-belief by the stories you've told yourself, probably for years and years, some of which you may not even be aware of. If you can believe that you are a spiritual being living a physical existence, then it's only a small step from there to knowing that this spiritual Self that you really are has none of the limitations that your physical Self has, such as illness or sadness or depression or lack of self-belief. When you tune in to that spiritual Self – with meditation or deep relaxation – then you are tuning in to the real you, the one that believes in you totally. When you connect more and more to that part of you, then you will automatically begin to believe in yourself and your power to achieve anything you set your mind to.

On rough days – we all have them – our self-belief dwindles. Often when this happens we can feel like we're sliding backwards, and we can even feel angry that we're losing a self-belief we worked so hard to gain. For a start, always remember that your record for getting through rough days so far is a hundred per cent.

Secondly, experience has taught me that if we are moving forward on the path that is our pursuit of purpose, then we will necessarily have 'bad' days as our heart, mind and soul expel the self-limiting beliefs and behaviours we are now moving beyond. We can feel pretty awful as old negativities exit. It's a good thing though, and to the extent we can, if we can really work at feeling happy when we're feeling awful, that old crap will move on more quickly.

Third, when we move in the direction of our purpose, the Universe steps up to aid us, and in so doing it can create a bit of a dust storm of uncertainty and greyness around us; if we understand the dull periods as the Universe working on our behalf, we can more readily accept those times as not really being about us and let go our attachment to self-limiting beliefs.

7.7 Take It Easy

- Be quiet.
- Listen to peaceful music.
- Slow down!

- Go for a walk.
- Get to the sea! (Or the mountains)

Be quiet.

1. Stop talking
2. Turn the radio off
3. Get out of the city
4. Turn your phone off
5. Go somewhere on your own
6. Stop thinking. Just stop it!

You know those people that just never seem to stop talking? Maybe you're one of them! I cannot *imagine* what is going on inside their heads. Makes me dizzy thinking about it. It's not good. Our world is a bit like being inside the head of someone like that. It doesn't shut up. And so we really need to *make* it shut up, to give ourselves any chance of finding quiet, especially if we generally live and work among a lot of this kind of noise. I used to live and work from my home in the countryside, I didn't have a television and nor did I have anything else on constant play, but I'm unusual in that respect. Most of the time these days, it's the same – I'm generally in the countryside and there's rarely much in the way of background noise.

If you're one of those people that talks all the time, this is not doing you any good. It's because your brain is not giving you a break and you think you have to get it all out. You don't. And you've just not picked up that everyone around you would really like it if you could shut up. I mean it. Everyone! They love you dearly but you're driving them nuts. But more importantly, you need to be quiet for your own sake. You cannot connect to the brilliant stillness of the Light, of the Divine, if your brain is in constant activity. You are less likely to enjoy moments of synchronicity and grace because your mouth is in the way of your heart and soul.

You will still your mind with regular meditation. Don't worry that you think you can't meditate, or that your constant thinking is preventing you from achieving any positive effects. It will work – it works for everyone – and your brain will eventually slow down. And when it does you will also enjoy the quiet more and not feel the need to fill it up with talking, television, and all the other noise. In fact you'll probably throw out your TV!

Listen to peaceful music.

They say cleanliness is next to Godliness but it's probably music. Don't listen to peaceful music you don't like though. Find what you do like.

This is not about listening to *any* music that you like – it needs to be something that's restful, that's going to allow you to be transported away in your mind.

180

You will have heard that Mozart is good for the mind; myself, I'll happily listen to *Four Seasons* by Vivaldi for hours. Maybe Tibetan drums or bowls do it for you. Gregorian chanting is amazing. Enya is beautiful. I've been transported away by my friend's album *An Abandoned Orchid House.* Experiment – ask your friends what they like – build up a library.

For me, indulging in some lengthy music like this is more a weekend thing; maybe it's an after-work thing, although for most households that can be a busy time. Invest in some good quality noise-cancelling headphones if you need to shut others out and/or keep your music to yourself.

Let the music take you where it will. Absolutely avoid wasting this time thinking about what went on at work today and what you're going to be doing tomorrow, or any kind of focused thought, especially if it has any kind of conflict at its centre. You'll defeat the purpose.

This is a time to relax. As well as letting your mind lightly wander, make sure you're comfortable – sitting or lying – and consciously relax every part of your body starting from one end or the other.

If thoughts of how indulgent this is come, or you starting thinking about what you *should* be doing, banish them. If they won't be banished, go do what you have to do and try again another time. If having these kinds of thoughts is always the case for you, then you need to work on getting rid of the thoughts, not the indulgence.

I recommend at least a half hour. More is better.

Slow down!

If you're always in a hurry the Universe can't get through to you. You won't hear it. It's like trying to speak to someone who's speeding past on a train. If you're lucky they'll pick up a couple of words. If you want to hear what the Universe intends for you and how it can help you, *you* have to slow down. Likewise, if you want the Universe to hear *you*, you've got to slow down so you can effectively communicate.

We don't develop our spiritual Self on the run. It just doesn't work that way, so if you think you can do that you're kidding yourself. You don't go to the gym for a 5-minute workout once a week and think it's sufficient to keep you fit and healthy. If you're really serious you do at least a half hour at least five times a week, and probably – to be fair and reasonable – you're going to do an hour, *and* you're going to do other things in-between, like walks and a healthy diet and so on.

The faster your life is going the *more* you will have to meditate in order to compensate: at least 20 minutes twice a day every day, with regular weekend retreats to stay in peak tune, as well as the exercise and diet regime, and much else. Easier to just to slow down and smell the roses.

Effective slowing down doesn't mean you get to blob out watching movies 24/7 either. A little of that may have some value, but real slowing down means meditating, pursuing creative projects, and getting outdoors.

Make a list of things you can add into your day that allow you to tune into your spiritual Self.

Go for a walk.

That might not be what you expected, or even what you wanted to hear. But it's one of the best things you can do. Truly.

There are three great reasons why a walk is helpful.

One is that it takes you somewhere different, and preferably into nature – walking by water is especially beneficial. Different is good. And walking somewhere different from last time is good. Every time you have a new experience you open your own personal energy to the fresh and the new, and every time you do that you open to the possibilities of the Universe. It's a great habit to get into.

Things almost never work out the way we think they will. When we create some kind of newness in our lives every day we're less likely to resist the changes the Universe wants to bring our way.

The second reason a walk is good, is that simply from a physical perspective, when we move our bodies, we're moving our Energy, we're flushing out the old, we're supporting our own physical well-being and thus every other aspect of our wellbeing: emotional, mental and spiritual included. All of our different aspects of Self operate as part of a team with all of the other parts – the more emotionally well we are, the more likely we are to be physically well, and vice versa. When we move we create Energy within and around us, and this is always a precursor to positivity.

The third reason is that for almost all of us, a walk – a bit like a shower – is an inspiration-generating action, especially if we're able to walk somewhere that has some particular natural or aesthetic appeal.

If you're literally unable to walk, or need assistance to take exercise, then do what you can to regularly create some activity that can produce this same kind of impact in your day-to-day life.

Get to the sea! (Or the mountains)

As far as I can tell, most people are either sea people or mountain people (or maybe bush people).

I'm a sea girl myself – I've always lived near it and I feel a little strange if I haven't seen it in a while. A lake just doesn't do it for me. It has to be the sea.

It refreshes and renews and inspires me. I get ideas, I get focused, I get relaxed, I get connected to the Universe. Literally the closer I get to the sea – like right in it! – the better it is for me.

I'm a little spoilt in New Zealand – most beaches are not even that crowded or built up, so you can walk for miles on a beach and never see another living soul! And the mountains and bush are much the same.

Whatever it is about nature that grabs you, go get grabbed by it regularly. Live near it if you can. It is a true expression of the Universe that has a rub-off effect on us if we let it. You cannot help but find more truth about yourself and your path when you regularly commune with the planet.

At the very least it will give your body and mind a rest from their usual daily tasks, and anything that takes you out of your usual routine, however briefly, helps to change the way you look at the world and your place in it.

At best you may just find the inspiration you're looking for.

> My soul is full of longing
> for the secret of the sea,
> and the heart of the great ocean
> sends a thrilling pulse through me.

Henry Wadsworth Longfellow

7.8 No Woman is an Island

- You cannot do it alone.
- Ask your friends & family.
- Talk to people you admire.
- Help someone.

You cannot do it alone.

On the one hand, it *is* all about you. On the other hand, no woman is an island, and everyone who comes your way is there to help you in some way on your journey. Make use of them. Find others.

My personal experience is that there's little of value in finding one particular guru or teacher; there is so much knowledge and wisdom

186

in the world today. There's an absolute tsunami of it, and so much of it is literally there for the taking. Listen and absorb what you can from every teacher that comes your way.

> I am not a teacher:
> only a fellow-traveller
> of whom you asked the way.
> I pointed ahead—ahead of myself
> as well as of you.
>
> *Bernard Shaw*

There is this idea that we have everything within us, and on one level that's true, but realistically few of us can access that and we need teachers and masters and coaches and so on to help us find the best that's in us. Don't be afraid of this but do give attention to your own intuition about what works best for you, and the type of teacher or coach that fits with your expanding view of the world. Over time your intuition will serve you better and better, as long as you use it – it won't develop if you don't use it, and that means making mistakes from time to time. Your courage will also develop the more you use it; don't be afraid to consider new ideas – there are so many, and they are there to serve us or not.

Ask your friends & family.

Sometimes when we start changing direction our best friends aren't on the same wavelength as us anymore, but here's hoping you have at least one friend around that you can talk to about where you want

187

to go, how you think you can get there, and literally what *they* think. If you are finding that some of your friends are just, well... not the people you want to hang out with so much in this regard, know that you're not alone – that's something that happens to a lot of people. Try to find at least one or two new friends who *are* on your wavelength and who're going along a similar path – you'll need them, and frankly they'll need you.

Having at least a couple of friends who get what we're on about is so important. You're treading new ground and you're going to want to explore that with others. Sometimes it's as simple as exploring recent thoughts with them; you'll probably find they've had similar ideas and so it'll be reassuring to find you're not crazy!

If some of your friends have been down some similar roads as the one you're embarking on, they'll be able to give you some of the benefits of their experience too. It can be hard to understand places we haven't been before, and like any traveller it's good to ask directions from time to time. We're not obliged to follow all of it, or even any of it. But if you trust your friends, at least listen, and mull it over with a view to understanding.

A lot of people can let their ego get in the way of taking advice. Everyone has something to teach you; when you give them the opportunity to do so, you validate their humanity and your own.

Always thank them – if it's not advice that suits you, that's fine, you can move on.

I've found a great deal of support and encouragement has come from various online communities I've joined, several that I've created myself. I've met many of my online friends in person now, so I'm not a believer in the idea that social media isn't real. The people you meet online are generally as real as you and I. Some of the friends I met initially online are now some of my best friends. If the friends physically in your world right now aren't on your journey, find others who are. It will be one of the best things you do.

Talk to people you admire.

If you ever get the opportunity to sidle up to someone *super* successful, then do it; but for most of us the opportunities are with the 'ordinary' successful, not to apply judgement to the idea of what makes one successful. Because it's important too that you realise the super successful are as ordinary as everyone else.

Pretty much everybody loves to tell their story if someone authentically asks them about it. And you learn so much from everyone's story, not the least of which is that they probably had to overcome many of the same obstacles you are facing. There is rarely anything so original about our own difficulties. And that's great news. Because they can all be overcome. That's one great reason to talk to other people about how they got where they got to, what they did to get there, and *why* they did what they did, and when. Many people are very isolated in their lives and it's incredibly valuable to talk to others who've succeeded in some way and find out how. Whilst there is camaraderie in hanging out with people who may be suffering similarly to us, there is a massive amount to be gained in spending time with people who are living their dreams, however modestly they might be going about it.

I know a lot of people who have made themselves invisible in their own worlds. Perhaps you weren't the favourite child, or you suffered some trauma in your past, or you've been given a lot of messages about how you're not good enough (by others or by yourself). As a result of these kinds of experiences, we learn to keep our heads down, we don't speak up, and even decades later we remain effectively invisible to many people around us who don't appear to appreciate us, who take us for granted, or perhaps who we feel look down on us in some way.

Make yourself visible! People love to share with other people, and when you take an interest in them then most of the time they'll take an interest in you too. But most of all, make yourself visible to people you admire. Every one of us is here to learn, so set about learning how others got to be doing what they do. You will learn something from everyone's efforts in their own life.

Help someone.

I usually tell people that the most important thing they can do for their life is meditate, but this one is arguably as important, or at least it's pretty up there.

There is a particular grace that comes to us when we give authentically and sincerely of ourselves to someone else. That grace descends upon us like a mantle for a while and at the very least we feel good about ourselves, perhaps invigorated, certainly positive. We have exercised our power to make a difference in the world and that power comes back to us multiplied.

Grace is a particular sweetness that puts us right in the Universe's view – in God's vision – in the grip of the Divine – for however briefly. It's an Energy to aspire to because it is loaded with inspiration, knowing and peacefulness. I believe this is one particular reason why helping others is so instructive in helping ourselves. It will also tend to spontaneously put us in a position of gratitude for our own life and the things in it, which is also an incredibly positive and useful position to be in in terms of manifesting more that is good in our own life.

8. Recognising Fear

> Who is more foolish, the child afraid of the dark
> or the man afraid of the Light?
>
> Maurice Freehill

Along with the obstacles of anger and depression and not forgiving, fear is equally our biggest obstacle to living our purpose. It comes in many shapes and sizes:

Fear of embarrassment

Fear of not having enough

Fear of the unknown

Fear of rejection

Fear of failure

Fear of success

Regardless of type, fears of all kinds have similar characteristics. There are many very good books written about fear that are far more comprehensive and far more useful than I can be here, but there are some points that I think are of vital importance in understanding how this relates to your purpose.

Resistance is futile: There are times when simply resisting fear helps you to move forward regardless and make some things happen. That can be important in the moment, especially if it's a situation that demands you act now. In general though, and taking a longer term view, it doesn't do to resist fear – particularly if that resistance involves running away from it. But suppressing it doesn't help either. It's better to take a look at the fear, break it down, understand it, learn from it. When we dissect fear it often just dissolves. Or at the very least we can be more informed as to why we respond with fear to certain things.

Courage: Aside from the notion of feeling the fear and doing it anyway, we need courage to look at and face our fears. It is one of the hardest things to do, to look at yourself, your perceived weaknesses, your shame, your anger… As I've already said, on the other side of fear there is almost always discovery, joy, success, surprise, happiness, and much more. When you do your personal work – dealing with your emotional 'stuff' – you remove blocks to your purpose flow and you gather courage to do more of this kind of work. It doesn't end, this personal work, but it does get easier. And as changes and happiness accrue in your life, you can become excited at the new challenges that will continue to turn up, because they all spell growth, as long as we continue to respond usefully to them.

Be in the Present: Fear is generally either based on a leftover from the past, or something from the future that hasn't happened yet and very likely won't. Fear keeps us in our comfort zones. Actually it keeps us in our discomfort zones too – the ones we've grown so familiar with that we can't let them go, because at least we know them, right?

> It is our very fear of the future that distorts the now that could lead to a different future if we dared to be whole in the present.
>
> Marion Woodman

To the extent that we can be here now, in this moment, in this time, we're better able to respond usefully to whatever situation – or more likely, opportunity – that is presenting itself to us.

Reality: Most fear is not based in reality. You've probably seen the acronym F.E.A.R. meaning 'false evidence appearing real'. We believe things are as they appear to be, often through several layers of our own perceptions. Or worse, through layers of prejudice. Reality isn't always the simplest thing to grasp – sometimes we're fearful for good reason – often though our fear is simply an illusion.

Danger is real;
Fear is a choice.

Will Smith

Confidence: Similarly, in the face of fear, we can also assume we're lacking some ability to respond effectively. We might think *I can't deal with that* or *I can't do that* and so we don't try. Confidence and courage go together – courage is doing it anyway, confidence is **knowing you have the resources for the task**.

Risk: As we get older we take fewer risks. In our youth we often took insane risks – I can well remember the speed and over-confidence with which I drove. But I also leapt into the unknown in ways I find less comfortable now – and that's from someone quite experienced in this kind of leaping. As we've acquired safety through career success and material acquisition, we can be less inclined to risk any of that. And so by middle age, we have this massive obstacle to our growth, and as a result our lives become narrower – *we* become narrower. We've blocked the opportunity for personal change. If you want a life that continues to expand rather than contract, you have to continue to take risks. You have to be prepared to risk what you believe you've acquired.

> If you let your fear of consequence prevent you from following your deepest instinct, your life will be safe, expedient, and thin.
>
> Katharine Butler Hathaway

Love: We might think courage is the opposite of fear, but actually it's love. Love is the language of our soul, of our purpose, of the Universe. Fear is the language of ego, of that which is not actually real. Much of the world we live in operates in the realm of fear and ego, and it's a challenge to operate and speak from a position of love

196

and spirit. But, like hate, **fear cannot survive in the presence of love**.

Pain: You will experience pain in facing your fears. It is the pain of ego putting up a fight It is a sign you need to face something, fix it, and move on. You've acquired baggage. We all do. There is nothing so horrible about you that someone else hasn't had to face in themselves too. Here are some hints that there's an internal battle going on between bullshit and reality:

- You're not happy. (Well, hellooo-ooo!)
- You're angry. A lot.
- You blame others. A lot.
- You judge others.
- You judge yourself!
- You think you're undeserving.
- People piss you off all the time.
- You complain about your life.
- Your personal relationships are in conflict.

If there is a meaning in life at all,
then there must be a meaning in suffering.
Suffering is an ineradicable part of life.

Viktor Frankl

I don't believe we are born to suffer. I believe we're here to experience joy. It just so happens though that **en route to joy we generally have to trip over ourselves several times** and that's painful.

9. The time is now

There are two 'Why now?' questions: one is: *why are you at this point now?* and the other is: *why do you have to do something about it now?*

Why are you at this point now? If you're reading this then it's more likely you're a woman (but if you're not, then *Hi!*), and you're most likely to be between 30 and 60. Partly that's because those are the main demographics of the people that follow my Facebook page, but also it's because this urgent need for purpose and meaningful work are an issue most particularly for that demographic.

A lot of people are waking up to the need to live life differently, and that will have different meanings and outcomes for different groups: maybe it means leaving the city, maybe leaving the rat race, maybe changing career, and a whole lot of other things. Middle-aged women often find themselves at a critical juncture in their lives that brings them to the question of their purpose: perhaps a relationship has ended, suddenly a long-term career is no longer satisfying, most particularly their children may have finished growing and left home. And as women of a particular age, we're seeing at an exponential rate what we can in fact *do*, and generally there's a huge desire to contribute. These changes aren't exclusive to middle-aged women of course, but it's that demographic that's more commonly in this state of urgency and desire about their purpose. As a generation, most particularly those of us in our 50s and 60s, we have manifested much of the equality our mothers fought for, and we're the ones who've broken most of the glass ceilings, or if we weren't the first to break it then we came along behind and greatly widened the hole. **Our own power is being revealed to us simply as a consequence of society's evolution of the last hundred years.** Many will experience this time as a *coming into your own power.* This is a hugely emotional, spiritual, often magical, frequently scary time. Don't let it go. Leap into it. It's beautiful and gorgeous and exciting and sometimes heart-breaking, and it's so worth it.

Why do you have to do something about it now? Because we're living in chaotic times, the world *needs* you to be living your purpose right now. It needs you at your best, and your best is what you'll deliver when you know why you're here.

The world is in a time of even more rapid development and evolution, much of it not always positive. Most of what I see, in that which is frightening and undermining of our freedom and sustainability, is what I personally believe to be the death throes of an unforgiving, abusive and self-loathing civilisation. And we are emerging from this into one that is open, creative and supportive. But we could always move there faster. And I'm sure we could get there with less pain along the way.

Which means that those who are awake to this newer, more purposeful way of life need to get on with it. Because it is up to us.

So many of us feel a sense of pressure. I'm not always good at responding to pressure but this is a kind of spiritual pressure that is calling us to rise up to the purpose of our higher selves and breathe life into that. And it's hard to ignore because it's the truth of who we are – we *are* those higher selves; desiring to live our own purpose and make the contribution we came here to make.

It's not a pressure like others you may feel in your life. It's not one to feel guilty about if you're not responding to it with full force. Guilt is not a part of Spirit. The pressure you feel is simply your Spirit and your purpose being felt by you. It is you tuning into them in ways you haven't before. It is you waking up. And that's super exciting.

> It seems like the chaos of this world is accelerating,
> but so is the beauty in the consciousness
> of more and more people.
>
> *Anthony Kiedis*

Postscript

As I've written and edited this book, I've sat in front of roaring fires in centuries-old stone and thatched houses in corners of paradise in Scotland, England, France and Wales; I've driven through the French and Spanish alps, and visited a dozen great cathedrals along the way; I've bussed through the Atlas Mountains, ferried about a Greek island, trained across Scotland, driven from the Himalayas to Delhi, and sailed the Hebrides; I've cared for twenty different dogs, several cats, a bowl of fish, and chickens with names of curries; I've stayed in hostels, B&Bs, retreat centres, a converted monastery, cheap hotels, 5-star hotels, and more than a dozen peoples' homes. I've eaten haggis and tagine, stuffed vine leaves and Yorkshire pudding; I've drunk sangria and cava, French wine and Edinburgh gin, Indian beer and Greek ouzo; I've been in roasting sun and an English winter; I've swum in the sea off Kefalonia, climbed a magic mountain in Wales, ridden a camel into the Sahara and watched the sun rise on the desert the next morning, walked stone circles in England and Scotland, danced in a music video with a bunch of hippies in Spain, explored 5,000 year old archaeological sites in the Shetlands and Orkneys, smelt the dye vats of Fez, kayaked the Isle of Skye, walked labyrinths in Chartres, discovered Guinness chocolate cake and goddesses in Glastonbury, visited a Tibetan Buddhist nunnery in the Himalayas, and I've visited more castle ruins, lochs, rivers, pubs and bookstores than I can remember or count; I hung out with an old friend I hadn't met before, several new family members I'd not known that long, a dozen travellers through Morocco for a week, fifty explorers aboard an expedition ship, both my children, and dozens and dozens and dozens of other gorgeous people from all over the world. And so much more.

This is my dream, to be writing, and traveling to places I love.

But it didn't happen overnight. It's been several years in the making. It started with one of the most radical decisions of all: to quit my job; to stop doing the thing I *thought* I loved, but that was really slowly killing me. And if it wasn't actually killing me, it was certainly destroying my soul. I had no particular idea at the time what my purpose was – I didn't even have it in my mind to *find* my purpose especially. I guess I had a sense that there was something else out there for me, and I decided to be unafraid of heading blindly towards it.

Time and time again I found the Universe stepped up to support me. More and more, I gave up on worry.

Along the way, I've done my personal work. I've wrestled some demons, and resisted others before eventually braving them. I've lost some friends but made a hundred times more new ones. People I've loved have left; others have turned up. I've learned a lot of things from a lot of people – I hope others have learned from me, and if not, I've tried to give what I could. Sometimes it was probably not enough and perhaps other times it was too much; I'm not given to keeping score.

I have few regrets but I do have some; mostly they are to do with having been less adequate as a mother than I would have liked, but as a friend once told me, you can only ever get a *C-* in parenting. I adore my children and their greatest gift to me is to be living their lives with passion and purpose. I would still cry all their tears for them if I could, but that's not how life works, and anyway they are both nothing if not very courageous.

I'm in my mid-fifties. I don't imagine retiring – it's a strange kind of word – but I can see sixty-five ahead of me (still my country's official retirement age) and I have a loose plan to spend the next ten years doing what I'm doing now. I am doing what I love, living a life I love, and I'm happier than I've ever been. I'm incredibly grateful.

Here is my best, most abbreviated advice:

Find what you love doing and do it.
Do your personal work.
Be brave.

And love whoever is around to be loved.

Appendix I

Purpose self-assessment ©

Give yourself a score for each item based on the scale below.

This applies to me:

1 = not at all

2 = not much

3 = neutral

4 = a bit

5 = very much

My Spiritual Beliefs

1 _____ I believe in something bigger than myself, and that that is of some influence in my life

2 _____ I believe we all have a purpose

3 _____ I have a regular spiritual practice

Section total _____

My Life

4 _____ I believe in making a contribution to the community/humanity

5 _____ I regularly take time to rest and reflect

6 _____ I create opportunities for new experiences, adventures or travel

7 _____ I have a healthy lifestyle (incl regular exercise and good diet)

8 _____ I'm generally happy **and** optimistic

Section total _____

My Work

9 _____ I love what I do

10 _____ I'm surrounded by people I respect and who respect me

11_____ I can be myself and I am free to speak my truth

12 _____ My work offers opportunities for learning & growth, without too much stress

13 _____ I feel purposeful in my work

Section total _____

My Goals

14 _____ I have goals, things I'd like to achieve in my life

15 _____ I review my goals regularly and set new ones

16 _____ I work on my goals consistently

Section total _____

My Relationships

17 _____ I'm happy in my key relationships

18 _____ I'm supportive of my partner, family, friends

19 _____ My partner, family, friends are supportive of me

20 _____ I listen to people, and offer understanding & encouragement

Section total _____

Me
21 _____ I'm grateful for what I have in my life

22 _____ I take calculated risks in the achievement of my life goals

23 _____ I don't shy away from challenges, I face up to things

24 _____ I'm quick to forgive others

25 _____ I go inward for solutions

Section total _____

Overall total _____

Scoring If any glaring gap comes up in one section much more than the others then that's obviously an indicator of where to put your attention going forward.

25 – 49 You may well be very unhappy with your life right now, you have no clue what your purpose is and you're most likely your own worst enemy. Your world may be very small and unexciting, and you see few, or no, opportunities for this to change. It's possible a lot of relationship issues, and the past, are holding you back. Your best path forward is to develop your relationship with your own Soul, and with the Creator/the Divine/Life.

Develop a daily spiritual practice (eg. meditation) and make sure you are living a physically healthy life. Seek friendships with people who have an adventurous spirit and a happy disposition.

50 – 74 You have a few things working for you and these will be important to build on. You may have some similar obstacles to those in the section above, and your path forward should be similar. Pick the section with the lowest *average* score (section total divided by number of assessment items in that section) and work on increasing that section by one average point. (eg. from 2.3 to 3.3, say). Don't try to work on everything at once; it's impossible.

75 – 99 You have some gaps but they're not insurmountable. You have the raw ingredients to be able to grow and develop in your life and purpose. Focus on the key spiritual elements as these will impact the other sections. Give attention to the section with the lowest average score. Take care not to undermine your own success and progress with self-judgement.

100 – 125 If you're not already clear on what your purpose is then you're well on the way to locating it just the same. You have most things in place to be able to live a happy and fulfilling life. Focus on building your daily spiritual practice to connect more powerfully to your purpose.

Re-assess your position in 3 months.

Appendix II
Introduction to Purpose

Buy it on Amazon https://amzn.to/2x7ZMNP

At some point in your life, I hope you'll ask the question either *what is my purpose?* or *what is the purpose of life?* They are the most important questions you can ask, since it indicates you have some sense that life has meaning other than that we are born, we work from nine-to-five, we acquire things, we have a little fun, and then we die.

If you should first of all ask me the question *does life* have *a purpose?* then my answer will be a resounding *YES!* It becomes entirely academic then whether there is a difference between *believing* there is a purpose and *wanting* to believe there is a purpose. **The reality is we are more satisfied when we are living a purposeful life than when we are not.** We are happier, healthier and our relationships are better; period. It's irrelevant if some people like to say that life has no purpose – it's meaningless to think this, since a purposeful life is a better, happier life to live. You can argue about that unscientific conclusion, but the evidence of a purposeful life has most certainly been concluded scientifically, so I for one am happily making the leap to believing that life has a purpose.

The purpose of life is to live a life of purpose.

So, what *is* the purpose of life? It's quite simple: it is to live a life of purpose. What is *your* purpose? It is taking what you love and what you're passionate about and making a difference; to make the world a better place by doing something you love. You may not even be very good at the thing that you're passionate about, although almost certainly you will become good at it if you love it enough.

Finding purpose though, and then living it, still seems to elude most of us. Even when we think we have it clear in our heads, it will escape sometimes and even trick us into thinking that's not it, that something else is 'it'.

So, there's finding your purpose, and then there's holding onto it. And then there are the times when your purpose *does* change.

In school, we're given the resources we need to pass exams to gain our high school qualifications. We are encouraged to think about what we're interested in and what we'd like to *be* when we leave school. If we don't think we're cut out for university or we're not interested in university, then most likely we're encouraged to *get a job.* If we do have some sense of a career – one that might involve tertiary study – **we are rarely if ever shown or told about this in terms of** *purpose.* *Job* or *career* are the overarching terms in use. And that's not surprising since *purpose* has definite connotations that are not generally a part of the lexicon of modern education or job and career-seeking.

Purpose goes beyond just what you're interested in. I'm interested in photography, but I don't want a career in it since it has no sense of purpose attached to it for me. I enjoy it, I appreciate it, I could even be quite good at it, but it's not my purpose. It *will* be someone's purpose – lots of people probably – but it's not mine.

Holding many of us in check is that on the way to achieving our purpose we all still have to pay bills, put food on the table, meet our obligations to our children, our communities and so on. This frequently – in fact almost always at some point – necessitates us having to do work that is *not* our purpose, but that supports us while we're going about working towards other goals. So it's worthwhile taking the view that **if it is getting us to where we want to be, it also forms a part of our purpose**, and there is little point in resenting it or hating it, even if we believe it is menial work that is somehow beneath us.

Your purpose will unfold with the positivity you put into your daily world.

Actually, there is no work that is beneath anyone; at least that is one important perspective to consider. As long as you take a negative attitude towards the work you do, you will find it takes you longer to escape the work you don't enjoy so much. Your purpose will unfold with the positivity you put into your daily world. If you practice happiness, you will work more quickly towards your larger goals. If you understand that the work you do now is helping you along the path towards your greater goals, then you will appreciate it, you will be better at it, you will be happier with it, and you will move more speedily in the direction of your dreams.

Unless we're fortunate enough to have some very unique kind of education or upbringing that teaches us we need to find our purpose, then we will usually come to this concept of purpose from one or both of two particular directions: either we have just always *known* somewhere inside us that we have a purpose; or we experience increasing frustration from the work we are doing, or from the nature of life about us and the stage of life we're at, and eventually hit on the idea that we lack purpose and we'd like to have some.

Whichever direction we come at it, we usually experience the need for purpose as a spiritual need. And by spiritual I do not mean religious, although for many these two are entwined. By spiritual, I am referring to a need for self-fulfilment – what Abraham Maslow[4] would refer to as self-actualization – that will often combine with a desire to make a contribution or to be of service in the world. It is a deep-seated need that arises from within and goes beyond intellectual or emotional fulfilment.

Maslow says "what a man can be, he must be"[5] and describes self-actualization in terms of achieving all that one can. I believe the desire for purpose goes beyond mere achievement and requires a connection to a higher self, to God, to the Universe, to destiny, or any similar concept that draws you into a realm that is greater than yourself. When I refer to *mere* achievement, I don't mean to say

---

[4] Maslow, A. (1954). *Motivation and personality.* New York, NY: Harper.
[5] Ibid. pp 91.

that achievements are not things to attain to; en route to achieving purpose we may complete a university degree, travel overseas, win an art competition, get married, get published in a prestigious journal, have a baby, and much more… all achievements that may bring satisfaction and pride. Such achievements may or may not bring with them a sense of purpose though, or they may bring a greater or lesser sense of purpose.

Possibly, once you have come to this idea of needing a purpose, you may feel this as quite an urgency. You may even feel frustrated or depressed at not having a purpose or not being able to figure out what your purpose is. **Definitely do everything you can to keep anxiety or frustration or depression from creeping in; none of these things will help you in uncovering your purpose, and indeed they will act as obstacles.**

Having a purpose though is not at all the same as finding a cause. Some people *will* find a cause to dedicate their life to; as often as not their motivation will spring from a personal tragedy or experience that compels them toward that end. Purpose, though, has much more to do with the ways we interact with the world around us, than in finding some particular organisation or issue to commit to.

There is no doubt in my mind that each of us as human beings has a purpose. I've not always been without doubt, but mostly I can say I've courted my doubts with a view to questioning my beliefs and where I've got to in my understanding; something I've tried to do throughout my life. I don't hold firmly to my beliefs in the sense that they define me; it is more the case that I have become aware of certain truths, and then only because my limited human senses grasp some small part of something far more complex than my tiny mind can know in full. I think this is the nature of much of what we think of as universal truths; some people with one view see one part of it and some people see some other part, and the groups can argue black and blue for generations because they think their limited minds have grasped the whole truth when actually this is very rare. **Those that have a larger view of any particular truth never fight about it.** So in this regard I don't have beliefs so much as I have some things I've seen and understood. Because my experience of the world and of learning has been reasonably broad and open, I believe I have a reasonably useful view that's worth sharing; feel free to take from it whatever works for you and discard that which doesn't.

This book has emerged from several areas of research and points of learning, and in large part from my experiences teaching, talking to and coaching others in the pursuit of their purpose over several years. My own pursuit of purpose has been a journey of many years, aided by the instruction I've received from coaches and spiritual teachers around the world. This is not everything there is to know about purpose, but it's a worthwhile amount of useful knowledge with some structure applied. Once this makes sense and you have absorbed this into your understanding, there will be more, so much more.

Throughout the book I will use the terms God, the Universe, the Divine, Energy, Source, the Light and other such terms; and they are used, from my perspective, more or less interchangeably. If one of these terms doesn't sit well with you for whatever reason, feel free to replace it with your own, or you could just not fuss about it too much and recognise that they are all just words to describe the one great Essence that animates all of life. When people have said to me *I don't believe in God*, I would often somewhat facetiously say *Poor God.* Others I know would say *well, God believes in you.* Mostly now I find it a pointless discussion; they are words and they are all lacking in some way in their ability to convey this extraordinary truth.

My experience in teaching and coaching on the topic of purpose has almost exclusively been with people who are definitely seeking to make a positive contribution to the world, to bring something of Light and beauty into others' lives. The term *Lightbearer* has been used to describe these people who are to all intents and purposes entirely ordinary. They are not gurus or great spiritual teachers, although some may become this. They are people with some talent (perhaps as yet unexplored and undeveloped), with a desire to be of service, with a need for meaning and Light in their own lives, albeit that for many that may just be some vague and undefined notion. There are millions of these people; they generally feel things deeply, and it seems to me that a lot more than half of them are women. They are the future of humanity, and they are seeking purpose and meaning, sometimes desperately. Many of them are youth, who find much of modern life, with all its cruelty and superficiality, a burden. They are rarely supported in their school system to explore the world in a way that suits their view of it, and sadly they are often not supported by their parents either in a manner conducive to their soulful development; and we know too well some of the downsides of this lack of support, in the alarming statistics of substance abuse, mental illness and suicide.

The widespread need to understand purpose seems more recent – a part of some new era that is exploding with information about new ways of living and experiencing the world and connecting with the Divine. While any one Faith or philosophy may be deeply fulfilling for any of its adherents, **no religion or body of learning has exclusive rights to the recipe for the good life**, and indeed much of new and popular learning has emerged from spiritual teachers wholly unaligned with a particular group. There is much to be gleaned; I hope this small contribution assists your journey.

Acknowledgements

I do most of my writing alone and unaided, but I couldn't do it at all without the affirmation and love of so many wonderful people who make a difference in my life every day. So here is an undoubtedly incomplete list – thank you all for your love and support and your many kindnesses:

My children, Madison and Ruby, and their dad, William; Katy, for being another (really great) mother to my kids; my father, Jim, who passed on while I was in the Himalayas last year – it seemed a good place to be; Kiwi soul sisters: Ra, Sue, Gillian, Theresa W, Dianne G, Angelique, Ann S, Karen C, AJ; Scots and English girls: Detta, Stacey, Claire, Fantastic Fe, and especially Jo who has sat through most of this; darling Americans: Doreen, Jenn, Ivy, Fiona C, Gayle W, Kathryn, Em, and so many others; Swati, you're in a class all your own; my Indian brothers, Frank and Puneet; my sister Tess; my Fitzmaurice cousins: Nicky, Catherine and Sue – god help us all that there are two Sue Fitzmaurices; to my many hosts in many countries, especially Gill, Gilli, Simone, Yvonne, Judi, Patricia, Elaine and David, Stacey & David, and many others; to darling Deb and Dai, two of the most wonderful people in my life ever; Sarah McCrum – you are always there for me – thank you for everything you've done; and last and far from least, my brother Ross, my best buddy and a miracle in my life.

Made in the USA
Columbia, SC
19 September 2018